Shay Pendray's
INVENTIVE
NEEDLEWORK

Published by

krause publications
An F+W Publications Company

700 East State Street • Iola, WI 54990-0001
715-445-2214 • 888-457-2873
www.krause.com

Please call or write for our free catalog of publications. Our toll-free number to place an order or obtain a free catalog is 800-258-0929 or please use our regular business telephone, 715-445-2214.

Library of Congress Catalog Number: 2003113743

ISBN: 0-87349-408-3

Edited by Barbara Case
Designed by Jan Wojtech

Printed in the United States of America

The following company or product names appear in this book:
Coats and Clark Button Craft Dual Duty, Coronet Braid by Rainbow Gallery, DMC, DMC Metallic Pearl #5, Dover Publications, Kreinik Braid, Lee's Needle Art, Inc., Lurex, Medici, Needlepoint Silk, Needlepoint Splendor, Santa's Beard, Saral Transfer Paper, Silk Mori, Silk Serica, Wisper, YLI Silk 100

DEDICATION

This book is dedicated to my grandchildren, Courtney Pendray, Connor Pendray, and Daniel Harwood. They are the national treasures of the future and I hope this book will be an inspiration to whatever their future endeavors may be.

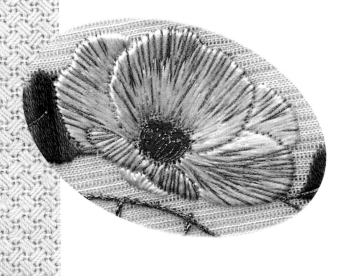

ACKNOWLEDGMENTS

I would like to give my heartfelt thanks to Jennifer Ashley Taylor for her wonderful photographs and her talent as a photographer.

Many thanks to my friends and students who were so willing to contribute to this book via their stitching.

- Diane Horschak, who stitches flawless Japanese embroidery and is an inspiration to all.

- Susan Kilkenney, Susan Beekman, Dorothy Goldstick, Eleanor Gibson, and Nancy Cox, who are so inspiring in their use of threads and stitches that make a painted canvas come alive.

- Sarah Warren, who has worked with me over 20 years and is one of the most wonderful people you could ever meet.

My thanks also extend to my long-time friend Dorothy Lesher for drawing the illustrations for this book. We have done many projects together and it is always a pleasure.

Lastly, I would like to thank my lifelong partner and husband Don Pendray for always being there for me. Don and our daughter Jody Pendray Harwood and son Peterson Pendray have given my life meaning and a desire to pass embroidery on to a new generation.

INTRODUCTION

Welcome to the world of needle arts. Before you start this adventure, I'd like to share how I came to be a stitcher and teacher.

I started stitching when I was 10 years old on a stamped cross stitch sampler. As a beginner I knew nothing of crossing all crosses in the same direction, or of stopping and starting, but I did know that I liked it. It was fun.

My primary and high school years were spent in a very unique learning environment. My husband Don and I attended school at Greenfield Village and Henry Ford Museum in Dearborn, Michigan. The village and living museum are comprised of approximately 50 historical buildings, all open to the public. This wonderful setting – with its village green, one-room schoolhouses, rustic town hall, and simple chapel – was where we earned our education from kindergarten through high school. Henry Ford, who regularly visited our classroom, created the village, museum, and the school dedicated to "learning by doing." Classes were held in historical buildings and one-room schoolhouses and we thought nothing of having historical samplers hanging on all the walls. I learned how to shear a sheep, then card, spin, and weave the wool, and use the resulting fabric to sew a garment. These skills were as basic a part of my education as reading, writing, and arithmetic. Using my hands and doing some form of handwork became second nature to me. Don and I have always cherished our education in a living museum and thank Henry Ford for giving us this rare opportunity to learn, which set me on the path of stitching.

While in high school I learned crewel embroidery, then took a class in creative embroidery. I loved it, and made great wall hangings to decorate my room. Then I discovered Hope Hanley's book, *Needlepoint,* and made a sampler of the stitches. I stitched each stitch on a piece of canvas and instead of writing the stitch name, I wrote the book page number where the stitch appeared. Consequently, I never learned the stitch names but I could tell you the page numbers. By this time Don and I were out of college, married with two children, and I was still stitching everything in sight. I loved doing it and loved to share it with others, so I opened a needlework store.

My thirst for learning took me to Scotland to study at the Glasgow School of Fine Arts where I learned about three-dimensional embroidery. I began to experiment with silk on canvas and working with metal thread. Then came the great adventure of traveling to Japan to learn Japanese embroidery from Master Saito, an absolute genius with color and design who had the uncanny ability to choose just the right technique to give the maximum effect with flat silk and Japanese gold thread. Japanese embroidery became the focus of my learning and I traveled some 18 times to study with four sensei (teachers) and learn this ancient art. This constant learning journey eventually led me to share the knowledge gained from 30 years of study and teaching.

I'm excited by this opportunity to encourage stitchers to try new and challenging techniques and to exercise their own creative talents. Don't be daunted by the seeming complexity of some of the pieces you see in this book. Every single one was done one step at a time. You can accomplish miraculous results by taking your time and giving each step the attention it deserves.

You will encounter a new challenge with each stitching project you begin. Start with a blank piece of fabric, look for an inspiration, translate the inspiration to paper, refine it, live with it a while, change it, walk away from it, come back to it, study it. Let it percolate in your mind. Color the paper design with colored pencils. When you are satisfied, transfer the design to your choice of ground fabric. Select the threads, choosing more than you anticipate needing. (When you are actually stitching, some of the threads may not work, so it is great to have a backup choice.)

Start to think about the stitches and techniques. Consult reference books. Try out stitches. If they don't work, consider it a learning experience. Do an easy part first, then come back to a part that may give you trouble. Whatever you do, enjoy the process.

Shay Pendray

TABLE OF CONTENTS

Section 2: Painted Canvas - 68

Chapter 6: Tools and Materials for Painted Canvas - 70

Chapter 7: Techniques for Stitching on Painted Canvas - 78

Chapter 8: Painted Canvas Examples - 89

Section 3: Shading - 99

Chapter 9: Tools and Materials for Shading - 100

Chapter 10: Techniques for Shading - 103

Section 4: Gallery of Designs - 121

GOLD WORK

Gold work is the ancient art of embellishing a cloth ground fabric with couched gold threads. Today, with the abundance of wonderful synthetic threads, gold work can be combined with needlepoint on canvas, added to clothing, or used in a revival of the traditional needlework. New methods of manufacturing have made the threads very accessible, affordable, and stitcher-friendly.

The origin of gold work is lost in time but in Exodus 39:2-3, you find the following reference:

"and he made the ephod of gold, blue and purple, and scarlet, and fine twined linen. And they did beat the gold into thin plates, and cut it into wires to work it in the blue and in the purple, and in the scarlet, and in the fine linen, with cunning work."

Gold work flourished in many areas of the world, and there are some distinct differences between European and Oriental gold work. The most obvious is that in Europe, the gold threads are couched with gold silk thread, while in the Orient the couching thread is orange-red. Another obvious difference is how the corners are turned. The Oriental corner has a very precise turn, while the European corner tends to be more rounded. Finally, in the Oriental style the work is a combination of silk embroidery stitches and couched Japanese gold or silver threads. The Europeans use these metal threads as well, but combine them with crimped wire threads such as bullions, crinkles, and pearl purl. Most of the examples in this book use a combination of the two styles.

CHAPTER 1:
TOOLS AND MATERIALS FOR GOLD WORK

The tools needed for gold work. From left to right, metric numbered triangles, needles, BLT laying tool, awl, koma, scissors, and button and craft lacing thread.

Threads

Most threads fall into two categories – *stitchable* and *nonstitchable*. Stitchable threads are threaded in a needle, then travel in and out of the ground fabric without damage or loss of shine to the thread. Nonstitchable threads lie on the surface and are held in place with a thinner thread. To pull them in and out of the ground fabric would damage the thread.

In needlepoint, thread is usually taken through the ground fabric, but in gold work not all gold threads are taken through the ground fabric – some are couched to the surface. Japanese gold and silver threads fall into the nonstitchable category with a few exceptions, which will be covered later. Their primary function is to add beauty to the piece.

Japanese Gold and Silver

Japanese gold and silver are wonderful, luxurious threads that can be used alone for dramatic effect or along the edge of a stitched area to enhance the motif. Their rich brilliance and reflective light play from different angles add great dimension and drama to the stitched work.

Japanese gold and silver differ from other threads in their construction and method of working. They are made by pounding gold or silver (or an alloy) very thin and adhering the metal to fine rice paper. The paper/metal combination is then cut into narrow strips and wrapped around a core of silk or nylon. Japanese gold and silver should be handled very carefully so you don't unwrap the metal/paper covering and expose the thread of the inner core. The gold covering should remain intact for maximum light play.

Japanese gold and silver threads are usually couched to the surface of the embroidery in *pairs of threads*. When you see a reference to couching Japanese gold thread around the edge of a motif, you can assume that this means couching a pair of threads. The threads are very seldom couched singly. When couched in a pair, the couching thread straddles the two threads (pair) at even intervals (see page 35).

Japanese gold and silver threads are sold both as imitation gold or silver or real gold and silver. Real gold is just

that – 24 karat gold pounded thin, adhered to paper, and wound on a core of silk. This thread will never tarnish and will always give off wonderful light play. Imitation Japanese gold and silver, which is more readily available and obviously less costly, is made from a Lurex adhered to paper and wound on a silk or synthetic core. Today's imitation gold is very realistic and very easy to work with. Historically, there was only real gold so the pieces you see in museums are usually done with real gold.

While in Japan I was fortunate enough to be invited to the house of a woman designated as a "National Living Treasure of Real Japanese Gold." This small woman appeared to be in her seventies. She had a table upon which rested a sheet of gold-covered paper that had been cut in strips. The strips were still attached at the bottom and top of the paper so she could pull them off one at a time. I watched in awe as she extracted a single strip about 36" long and wound it around a core of silk. The core silk thread hung from the ceiling and as she wound the real gold around it, she wrapped it on a shuttle for safekeeping. The process of making the thread was done completely by hand and from there it went to only the very best stitchers in Japan. I was mesmerized by the woman, who obviously had done this for many years. I watched for two hours, fascinated by how she twisted the paper onto the silk core. I never could see how each individual paper was fastened to each new paper so seamlessly but felt it was a great privilege to have witnessed the process.

Today, imitation Japanese gold and silver threads are so well made that you have to look carefully to tell the difference from real. But when you actually couch with both types, it is easy to tell the difference – real gold thread is much easier to work with. When you are starting to learn gold work, imitation is just wonderful; when you are very experienced and doing a major piece, there is nothing like real gold.

Japanese red couching thread and spools of YLI #100 silk. They both work successfully for couching.

Japanese gold and silver threads come in sizes 1 to 15. Size 1 is the smallest and is the basis for each number after that. For instance, size 2 is two times the diameter of size 1; size 3 is three times the diameter, and so on.

Sizes 1 and 2 are small enough to be threaded in a needle and passed through the ground fabric, so they are considered stitchable threads. They should be threaded into a needle that will let them travel through the ground fabric without damaging the thread. If you hear a tearing noise while stitching, change to a bigger needle.

Sizes 3 through 15 of Japanese gold and silver are nonstitchable threads that are couched to the ground fabric with couching silk, a very fine twisted silk thread.

Couching Threads

YLI Silk Thread #100 works beautifully as couching silk and is available in a variety of colors from most sewing stores. Japanese couching silk is available in red, white, gold, and a few other colors. This thread can be found in specialty needlework stores. For special effects in couching, twisted silk threads such as Needlepoint Silk can be used as couching silk. Needlepoint Silk can be purchased in needlepoint stores in small skeins and comes in a great variety of colors, which is an

---

Hint

Thread size 1 or 2 Japanese gold into a chenille needle, take a few stitches near the selvage, then examine the thread. If the core shows or the paper covering has moved, use a larger needle. (A chenille needle is a sharp needle with a large eye. The eye is usually the same size as in a tapestry needle.)

Check purl, a metal thread from the bullion family. This is a very delicate thread that will stretch out of shape if not handled carefully. It is cut into pieces, then a hollow core is threaded on the needle and stitched on the ground fabric as you would a bead.

Rough purl, another example from the family of bullion metal threads.

Gold pearl purl comes in various diameters and is couched on the surface of the embroidery.

advantage when you want a special effect.

There are two schools of thought about the color of the couching thread. Oriental gold work is usually couched with red-orange couching thread, while English gold work is usually couched with gold couching thread. Oriental stitchers believe the red-orange enriches the gold color and the English believe the couching threads should recede into the work.

Gold workers sometimes wax the couching threads for added durability and strength. I don't usually wax my couching thread because the wax attracts dust and can soil the work. In the Orient only pure, colorless vegetable wax is used on the silk couching thread. They believe that the colored beeswax slightly changes the color of the silk

couching thread. English work is usually waxed with beeswax.

In Oriental gold work, Japanese gold and silver are couched and that is usually the only technique used. Occasionally stitchers use a twisted gold and silver but the majority of gold workers use only Japanese gold or silver. In English gold work, they couch but also tend to use more types of threads such as bullions, crinkles, etc.

Bullions

Bullions (also called purls) are a family of nonstitchable threads made of wire twisted closely together, coiling to form a hollow center. Bullions are very delicate to work with and must be handled with care. If you pull on the finely coiled wire it will not return to its original position and often has to be discarded.

A thick metallic that is used in areas where a wide thread is couched.

Two types of metallic braids. Both are couchable and stitchable.

Bullions come in different diameters and colors and are usually sold by the yard or meter. Sometimes the real gold threads are sold by the inch. If they are made of real gold, they can be very expensive, but imitation threads work just as well and are fun to use.

The bullion family can be broken down into faceted check purl, smooth purl, and rough purl. Each one is treated the same way. They are cut into small pieces that are threaded onto a needle (just like you would thread a bead) and stitched to the ground fabric.

Bullions are never couched because the stitching process would crimp and damage the bullion. Use bullions sparsely on a project for great interest. They make wonderful antennae, tear drops, borders, and centers of flowers.

Bullions are sold in specialty shops and come in vari-ous gold shades and colors (if you are lucky enough to find them). Newer bullions don't tarnish because they have a low metal content.

Pearl Purl

Pearl purl, also called jaceron, is a crimped wire that doesn't have a hollow core. It is constructed much more firmly than bullion. Pearl purl is highly coiled and can be used in the tight coil or can be stretched and relaxed to open up the coils. Once pulled and stretched, it will not return to its original shape. It is a non-stitchable thread.

Pearl purl is usually referred to as a metal thread because it has some real gold content. It is couched to the surface of the ground fabric and never taken to the back of the fabric. It makes a beauti-ful crinkled-looking outline around a shape.

Pearl purl comes in size 3 small, 5 medium, and 8 large, and is sold by the meter or yard. If it has a high real gold content, it can be sold by the inch. Pearl purl is available in three colors – silver, gold, and copper. You can purchase it at independent needlework retailers.

Twists

In twists two or more metallic strands are twisted firmly together. The diameter of the strands can vary, so some fine twists are stitchable while thicker ones must be couched to the ground fabric.

One example, DMC Metallic Pearl #5, comes in gold and silver and is espe-cially handy because it can either be couched or stitched on needlepoint canvas or silk ground fabric. On silk, you must use a needle that will make a hole large enough for the metallic thread to pass

Examples of the wide variety of silk threads available today.

Gold crinkled thread.

through without resistance. If you hear a squeaky noise while stitching, use a larger needle.

Braids

In a braid, several metallic threads are braided together to form a single thread.

One example is Coronet Braid by Rainbow Gallery, which can be couched in place or stitched in a variety of needlepoint stitches. It comes in different diameters, starting with the smallest size 4, and going to sizes 8 and 16.

Kreinik braid can also be a stitchable or nonstitchable thread, depending on where

it's used in the design. It can be couched to form a beautiful edge or stitched in a textured needlepoint design. It comes in different diameters ranging from small size 4 to large size 32.

Crinkles

Crinkles are created by winding a flat metallic strip around a thread core so tightly that it crimps. Crinkles are nonstitchable and are usually couched in single threads, with the couching threads in every other valley.

Crinkles make a very beautiful undulating outline on a motif. They are always attached to the surface, never taken to the back of the work.

Silk Threads

Stitchable silk threads are used to enhance gold work. They can range from flat silk (reeled silk, never spun) found in Oriental embroidery, to twisted silks such as Splendor and Needlepoint Silk. Silks are usually an adjunct to the gold work.

Flat silk is the most luxurious and gives the utmost in shine and light play but is the most technically challenging of the silks. One strand of flat silk is a combination of 12 *suga*, which is the filament that is unwound from a single silk cocoon and is the diameter of a spider web strand. Twelve cocoons are unwound at the same time and the suga combined to form one continuous thread. These threads are combined to make flat silk. With skill, flat silk can be divided into suga and worked with in increments as small as two suga. Thread this fine gives the stitcher the ability to have intricately shaded animals and flowers and the utmost in color variation.

Flat silk comes in 400 colors, divided into color families, and is sold on spools in 40- or 50-yard lengths. It is available at a handful of independent retailers and is used by skilled embroiderers.

Splendor and Needlepoint Silk are readily available from needlepoint stores and are fairly easy to work with. Because of their twists, they do not illicit as great a shine as flat silk but they are much easier to work with.

Splendor is wrapped on cards, sold in many colors divided into families, and is widely available. It is a 12-stranded silk that can be stranded and stitched using all 12 strands or just one strand. It is a friendly thread to work with and its wide range of colors gives the stitcher great latitude.

Needlepoint Silk is made in China and twisted into hundreds of colors divided into color families. It is sold in five-yard skeins and larger hanks with over 40 yards of thread. It is readily available and is also very user-friendly. Needlepoint Silk is a great choice for needlepoint and can also be used for embroidery. Because of the twist, it does not give off the light play that you find with flat silk.

Fabrics

Japanese Fabrics

I have dabbled in many types of embroidery – hardanger, white work, crewel, cross-stitch, and needlepoint. I have never met a painted canvas I didn't like. I love stitching all of it, but when it comes to stitching toward perfection and to fill my soul, I always turn to Japanese embroidery. I have been known to become so engrossed in my work that I stitched for eight or 10 hours. The challenge of the flat silk, the challenge of the edge – each stitch is a new adventure.

During my years of stitching, I always wanted to develop a method where different varieties of stitching could be combined in one piece to complement each other. In the past, I designed and stitched primarily on needlepoint canvas, which allowed me to use precise counted stitches and do wonderful geometric stitching. When I traveled to Japan, I discovered the freedom of stitching on fabric. With fabric, I could put my needle anywhere I wanted to, not just in a hole. This led to more creative stitching but also forced me to make a decision with every stitch. No longer did I have the comfort of knowing which was the right hole – I had to choose where the needle would go down. This increased the challenge of the embroidery and opened up great possibilities. I grew to like this freedom, but also missed the precise stitching of canvas work. I wanted to combine the techniques but didn't know what ground fabric would be suitable. Needlepoint canvas was great for counted work but I couldn't pierce the threads as minutely as I wanted to. Linen and other counted fabrics worked for counted and uncounted stitches but could be rough on flat silk threads.

In Japan, Master Saito introduced me to Sha, a leno woven silk ground fabric with closely woven holes. Sha is countable, but the holes are tiny, so I could use wonderful silk threads such as flat silk and do embroidery stitches in combination with counted stitches. Discovering this ground fabric led me to a whole new method of stitching. Now I can count but also stitch with freedom, without adhering to the holes. Because Sha is 100% silk, I can travel silk threads through the ground fabric without roughing the thread.

Master Saito firmly believed that silk threads (he used flat silk) should not be used on any ground fabric except silk. Using silk thread on canvas was not acceptable to him. (If you try flat silk on canvas, you'll understand why he felt that way.) However, he was not privileged

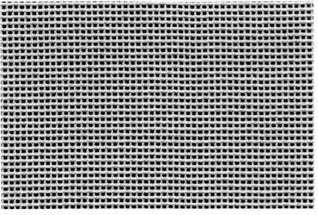

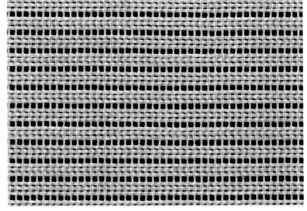

Silk Sha fabric. Note that it is not a true even weave.   *Silk Ro ground fabric.*

to have access to today's wonderful twisted silks that glide through canvas without damaging the silk.

I also learned about Ro, uneven Ro, and Ra fabrics. All of these ground fabrics are silk and can be counted in some way, but can also be used as embroidery fabric. All four fabrics are elegant members of the gauze family known in Japan as *karami ori,* or "loose open mesh." These fabrics are used in kimonos and in over-robes for Buddhist monks. The warp threads are twisted in pairs and the weft threads are inserted between the twists to form an open fabric that is very strong, beautiful, and cool to wear.

Japanese fabrics are not readily available but can be purchased in specialty stores. They are 14" wide, sold in obi lengths (14 meters) or kimono lengths (17 meters), or by the running inch for embroidery projects. A piece as small as 10" is sufficient to do a small motif. Don't expect to cover the whole ground fabric with stitching because the fabric is so beautiful that much of it should be exposed to make the most of that beauty.

Naturally, if you are just starting out or are an inexperienced stitcher I would not expect you to use one of these fabrics. Visit your local fabric store and buy a good, substantial silk or combination of silk and manmade fiber. Many of these fabrics are wonderful to work with and come in a world of colors. Avoid buying thin fabrics like china silk or silk lining. Fabrics this thin cannot support the gold work.

Sha Fabric

Sha appears woven like needlepoint canvas but is not a truly even weave. Usually the horizontal (weft) threads are closer together than the vertical (warp) threads. Sha can't be stitched in basketweave or diagonal stitches, but it works very well for upright or cross-stitches. Silk Sha is very easily stitched with a sharp needle, and so lends itself well to embroidery stitches such as long and short. Because it can be counted and/or used for freeform stitching, it offers the best of all worlds.

Sha is woven in different counts, as low as 30 threads per inch to as high as 42 or 50 threads per inch. The silk threads are even and clean and the holes are fairly large, which makes them easier to see than on 24-count congress cloth. Sha is 14" to 15" wide and comes in 14-meter rolls. It is also sold by the running inch and can be purchased at specialty stores. It is comparable in price to a very good piece of silk fabric.

Ro Fabric

Ro is an even weave fabric. It has a row of holes, then multiple tightly woven weft threads, then another row of holes. This sequence of holes and threads is woven in a repeat pattern and the stitches are usually upright stitches, stitched in Bargello-type patterns.

This fabric is often embroidered with summer flowers and water motifs to

Silk uneven Ro ground fabric.

Silk Ra, which is a combination of woven patterns and Sha.

give an even cooler feeling in the hot summers of Japan.

Ro fabric is sold in specialty stores by the yard or running inch and comes in 14" to 15" widths. It is comparable in price to a very good piece of silk fabric.

Uneven Ro Fabric

Uneven Ro is also used for cool summer kimonos but is woven in an uneven pattern. It is constructed of horizontal rows of holes, several tightly woven threads, a row of small holes, then several rows of tightly woven weft threads. In Ro, the distance between the tightly woven threads and the diameter of the holes remains the same. In uneven Ro, the distance between the rows of holes varies, as does the diameter of the holes.

Uneven Ro can be stitched in counted upright or cross-stitches, Bargello patterns, or embroidery stitches, and offers much flexibility in the stitching. "Morning Glories" on page 101 is stitched on uneven Ro fabric.

Uneven Ro is sold in specialty stores by the yard or running inch and comes in 14" to 15" widths. It is comparable in price to a very good piece of silk fabric.

Ra Fabric

Ra is the most complicated woven fabric. The warp threads create intricate designs by running at diagonal angles to the weft. Ra is the ground fabric used for the "Golden Leaves" design on page 49. On that piece of Ra fabric, five different intricately woven patterns form different leaf motifs. The fabric itself dictated the embellishment and led the stitching along.

Ra is definitely a specialty fabric that is not readily available but is shown in this book because of its uniqueness and its amazingly creative structure. Special weavers create these fabrics and they weave new patterns often, rather than repeating old patterns.

This type of ground fabric allows the combination of needlepoint stitches, Japanese embroidery, and surface embroidery techniques. These fabrics are difficult to find, but if you do find one, envision following the lines of the woven motifs with gold threads to enhance the already existing patterns.

Needles

Tools and Accessories

Koma

Gold work requires few needles because most of the threads are not stitchable. However, you do need a couching needle. A #9 or #10 crewel needle works well, as does a size 2 or 3 machine-made Japanese couching needle. These have very small eyes and a novice would be better off with the #9 crewel. You can also use a very small quilting needle.

A #24 chenille needle works fine for constructing a sinking needle (see page 39 for instructions).

Use #22 and #24 chenille needles for braids and twists on noncountable ground fabrics and #20 or #22 tapestry needles for the same threads on countable ground fabrics.

Koma are small spools on which you wind metallic thread. I highly recommend that you use koma if you are couching metal threads (Japanese gold or silver). Koma can be used with any metal or metallic thread that is couched but are used primarily for Japanese gold and silver and sometimes with braids and twist. They are used only in the couching process and are only suitable for threads that are going to be laid on the surface of the work.

Koma are sold in pairs at independent needlework shops and are under $20.

The benefits of using koma with Japanese threads are:

• When using koma, you will seldom need to put your hands on the thread, thus protecting it from skin oils that could remove the shine.

• Winding thread onto koma adds a beneficial overtwist to the thread. As you couch and unwind the thread from the koma, some of the overtwist is eliminated and if you remove too much overtwist, the thread core will be exposed, which is not desirable. If you attempt to couch a pair of threads by laying them on the surface without using koma, you will have to continually add overtwist to the thread to prevent the core thread from showing. This manipulation with your hands will soil the metallic and could damage the thread. Koma allow you to minimize contact between the thread and your hands.

• The weight of the koma keeps the thread exactly where you want it as you are couching. This gives you a great advantage when you are turning a corner, rounding a circle, or forming intricate motifs because you can move the koma ever so slightly and they stay in place while you make the couching stitch. You can continue to move them to form perfect shapes. This fine manipulation of the pair of threads can't be accomplished when just placing the pair on the surface and moving them by hand to couch.

• Japanese silver or gold threads are normally couched in pairs and the koma keep the two threads side-by-side.

(Instructions for winding Japanese silver or gold on koma are on page 33.)

Laying Tool

A laying tool is primarily used with multiple strand stitchable threads such as Needlepoint Silk and Splendor Silk. They are available at most stores that carry needlework supplies.

A laying tool straightens multiple strands so they lay side-by-side for maximum light play and beauty. A laying tool should have one sharp end so the threads slip off easily and one square end so the tool fits

comfortably in the palm of your hand without rolling around. The square end also allows you to lay the tool on your work without it rolling off. A laying tool is also great for reverse stitching – the sharp point is perfect for picking out stitches.

(Instructions for using a laying tool are on page 81.)

Tweezers and Scissors

When working with Japanese gold and silver you might need to pinch the corner or take hold of an end of the thread. Small precise tweezers that are compact and easy to handle can move the gold or silver threads without damaging them. They are also handy to have around your canvas work when you need to pick out threads. In English embroidery, tweezers are referred to as "burling irons."

There are many types of scissors on the market and most stitchers have a favorite. For gold work, you should have scissors that you use just to cut the metal threads. Metal will dull regular embroidery scissors so you need one pair of scissors for regular threads and one for metal or metallic threads. Snip type scissors work best for metallics because they have a very sharp point that can be directed to the minutest piece of metal. They are very sharp and hold their edge very well. I have used the same pair for several years with great success.

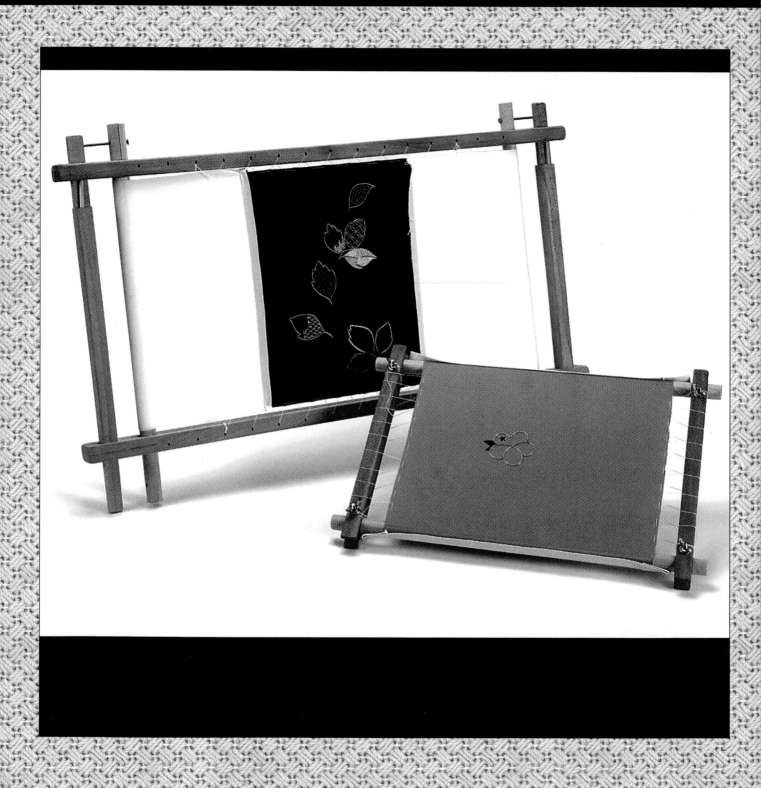

When framing up for gold work, remember that you are framing up ground fabric, not cross-stitch fabric or needlepoint canvas. Consequently, the framing up process is different because the ground fabric must stay trampoline tight throughout the whole stitching process to ensure a beautiful finished piece. Therefore, you will spend much time and energy on the framing up process. I set aside a good two hours for framing up on a Japanese frame.

For gold work, I prefer to work on Japanese frames but they are twice as expensive as roller frames and the cost difference may be a factor in your decision, especially if you are not sure you will do multiple projects in gold work. Japanese frames have been used for 1,600 years and have been perfected to keep ground fabric much tighter for a longer period of time. Don't worry if you prefer a roller frame — you'll get a good tight fit with either.

Both Japanese frames and roller frames will last a lifetime. If you are a stitching nut like me, you will likely have multiples of both. Roller frames and Japanese frames have specific ways of framing up. Take time with each step to ensure that your embroidery will have the very best foundation. The more accurately you frame up, the better your end result will be. If your frame is too loose, the gold threads will not be in smooth even lines when you remove the piece from the frame. Loose ground fabric is too spongy to hold the heavier gold threads.

You are probably familiar with embroidery hoops and may be tempted to use one. Don't! Hoops are never used for gold work for several reasons. First, with an embroidery hoop, you must frame and unframe your work during the stitching process. This framing and unframing will ruin gold work. Secondly, the hoop will crush the gold threads.

I've seen stitchers who lace artist stretcher bars and tighten the ground fabric on them. In my estimation the stretcher bars don't keep the ground fabric tight enough. I feel very strongly that framing up correctly makes the end product better and the stitching process easier.

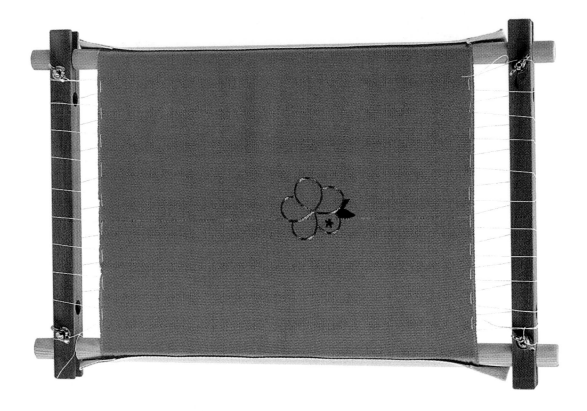

Framing Up on a Roller Frame

A good roller frame is suitable for gold work as well as for needlepoint, cross-stitch, painted canvas, and embroidery. Roller frames are easy to find at stores that carry needlepoint or needlework supplies. They consist of four parts – two sidebars with nuts and bolts, and two side dowels with attached twill tape. When choosing a roller frame, examine the twill tape. If it isn't the highest quality, don't purchase the frame. Each stitching project will be sewn to the twill tape either by hand or machine, and if the tape won't take multiple sewings and rippings, the frame will not last a lifetime. The frame must also be able to tighten enough so that the fabric is trampoline tight.

1. Cut a piece of ground fabric and mark the selvage sides "east" and "west" and the remaining two sides "north" and "south." If one of the east/west sides is the actual selvage, the other side is probably a raw edge. To prevent this raw edge from raveling, zigzag, backstitch, or cover the edge with white artist tape (masking tape usually doesn't stick well enough). It isn't necessary to do anything to the selvage edge.

2. Mark the centers of the north and south edges of the fabric.

3. Measure the twill tape on the roller frame and use a pencil to mark the centers of both the top and bottom tapes.

Fig. 1. Attach the fabric to the twill tape.

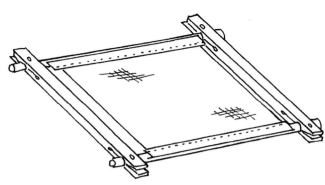

Fig. 2. Sew fabric to the twill tapes at the north and south.

4. Line up the center of the twill tape with the center of the north edge of the fabric. Place the fabric under the twill tape on the rod. The fabric will be between the tape and the wooden rod as shown in Fig. 1. Pin the fabric to the twill tape.

5. Sew the twill tape to the fabric either by hand or with a sewing machine. (Fig. 2) If you are using a sewing machine, place the wooden rod of the frame to the left of the presser foot and sew all the way across along a thread line on the fabric. Backstitch at both ends to lock your stitches. If you are sewing by hand, use a double thread or strong thread like buttonhole twist and backstitch across, being sure to follow the same thread. This creates an even tension when the canvas is stretched.

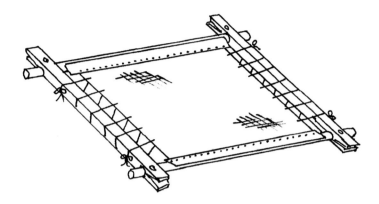

Fig. 3. Lace both sides of the fabric to the frame.

Hint

Don't put the fabric on top of the twill tape or you won't get the correct pull and your raw threads will be exposed and constantly snag as you stitch.

6. Repeat sewing the fabric to the twill tape on the south end.

7. Insert the tape rods in the ends of the end bars and rotate the rods at the top and bottom until the fabric is trampoline tight and secure. Tighten the nuts and bolts.

8. Lace the edges for greater tension. (Fig. 3) Thread a sharp needle with sturdy thread (carpet thread or buttonhole twist). Tie the end of the thread to a bolt on the frame or around the side bars as shown. Make a stitch by taking the needle down through the ground fabric. Carry the thread up, over, and around the side of the frame, then repeat the stitch. Continue until you reach the end of the bar. Go back and tighten the thread.

You may have to go back several times for sufficient tightness. Tie off the thread around the bar or around the bolt on the frame. Repeat the lacing on the other side of the frame.

Hint

If you are using the roller frame for canvas work or cross stitch it is not necessary to lace the edges. However, for gold work lacing is a must.

9. Each time you sit down to work, test the tightness of the fabric – it should always be trampoline tight. If not, tighten it.

Framing Up on a Japanese Frame

Japanese frames are the ultimate for maintaining tightness. They are not generally used in canvas work but could be very easily. I have seen these frames in Japan, China, and Korea. They are the primary frame for Oriental embroidery. Their great advantage (and the reason most embroidery stitchers prefer them) is that they keep the ground fabric very tight.

English gold workers use what is called a slate frame. These are extremely hard to find in the United States. I have several and have used them very successfully for embroidery projects. Slate frames are more adaptable to different sizes of ground fabric than Japanese frames. Japanese frames are made to accommodate Japanese fabrics, which are usually only 14" to 15" wide and can be as long as 17 meters, which means that you can only use fabrics up to 15" wide. The fabric length can vary greatly because it is rolled around the shuttle poles.

Japanese frames come in three sizes – small (18" x 19"), traditional (30" x 19"), and large (40" x 20"). The traditional size is the most used of the frames. You can find Japanese frames in specialty needlework stores.

Japanese frames consist of two horizontal bars, two pair of shuttle poles (split dowels), two weft bars, two nails, and one pair of chopsticks. (Fig. 1)

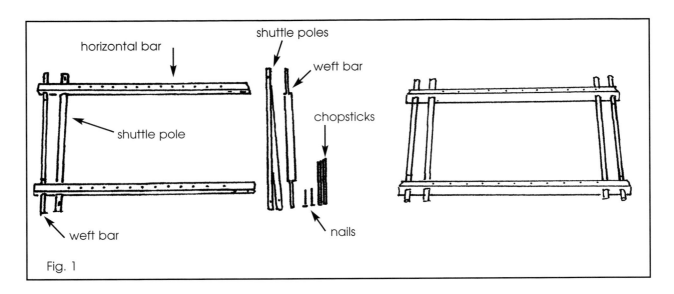

Fig. 1

Hint

Japanese fabrics are about 14" to 15" wide, selvage to selvage, so the fabric you frame up on a Japanese frame should be this width. If you need to cut off one selvage to create this width, zigzag stitch the raw edge to prevent raveling. The length of the fabric can vary.

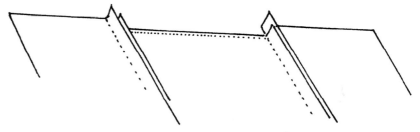

Fig. 2. Sew extra fabric to each end of the ground fabric.

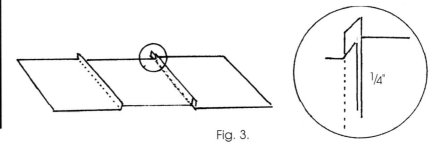

Fig. 3.

Assembling the Frame and Fabric

1. Sew extra fabric to the two end raw edges of your ground fabric. (Fig. 2) For this border fabric, choose a strong, white, high grade of cotton (no fabric blends - they stretch too much). If you're tempted to use sheeting, don't. It is not strong enough. Sew the additional fabric to each warp end of the ground fabric, using a 5/8" seam. Be sure to sew along a single weft thread of the ground fabric and backstitch at the beginning and end for at least 1". This is more easily done with a sewing machine but can se sewn by hand (be sure to backstitch).

The additional fabric should extend about 1/4" beyond the ground fabric at all four corners. (Fig. 3)

Hint

If the ground fabric has no selvage, machine stitch 1/4" from the north and south edges to reinforce the fabric for the lacing procedure you'll do later.

2. Place one horizontal frame bar in the north position and the remaining horizontal bar in the south position. Make sure the lacing holes in the horizontal bars face inward (facing each other).

3. Check the split shuttle poles to make sure the nail holes line up on the pairs. Slip the two sets of shuttle poles into the round holes of the horizontal bars.

4. Insert the weft bars into the rectangular holes on the horizontal bars.

5. At this point the frame is very precarious and can fall apart easily. Carefully place the frame in a frame holder. Use a frame holder that will hold the frame by both weft bars. A frame holder that will hold only one side of the frame won't work. If you don't have a frame holder, suspend the frame between two tables or take the leaf out of a table and suspend the frame in the middle of the opening. To accomplish the next step, the fabric must drop between the shuttle poles. (Fig. 4)

6. Remove the top half of the right-hand shuttle pole and place it to the right of the frame. Use a permanent marker to mark this top half with "rt." Mark the other half of the same shuttle pole with "rt" so you'll always know which halves go together. Remove the top half of the left-hand shuttle pole and place it to the left of the frame. Mark each half of this shuttle pole with "lt."

7. Place the fabric on top of the bottom half of the shuttle poles. The selvage of the fabric should run parallel to the horizontal bars. Frame the fabric with the seam side up to prevent any raveling from getting into the back of the work. The warp threads of the fabric run east and west. Allow the fabric to droop at least 6" between the shuttle poles. If the fabric

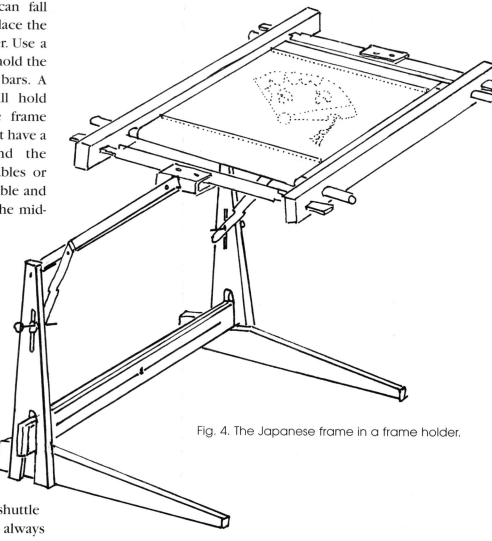

Fig. 4. The Japanese frame in a frame holder.

doesn't reach from shuttle pole to shuttle pole, or doesn't droop 6", add extra fabric to each nonselvage side of the fabric. The ground fabric plus the extra fabric should extend out from the shuttle poles on each side by at least 6".

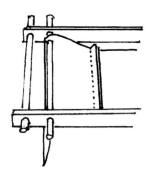

Fig. 5. Shuttle pole.

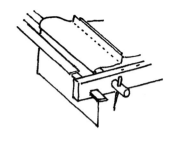

Fig. 6. Insert the nails facing downward.

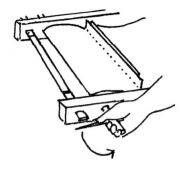

Fig. 7. Turn the shuttle pole nail 1¾ turns to under the weft bar.

Hint

If you are using silk ground fabric that is long enough without adding additional fabric, you should still place protective cotton on top of the silk where the shuttle pole will rest, to prevent damage to the silk ground fabric.

8. Slide the upper half of each shuttle pole back in place. (Fig. 5)

9. Insert the two nails *pointing down* into the holes of the shuttle poles on the near side of the frame. There are four sets of nail holes – two on each end of the shuttle poles – but you will only use the two nail holes nearest you on the same side of the frame. (Fig. 6)

10. Adjust the fabric so it is equidistant between the shuttle poles and still drooping at least 6". Make sure the extra fabric edge is an equal distance from the horizontal bar on both shuttle poles.

11. With the nails pointing down, start at either end of the frame and turn the shuttle pole nail outward exactly 1¾ turns of the nail. End with the nail pointing under the weft bar. Slip the weft bar over the nail to prevent the nail from turning further. (Fig. 7)

12. Do exactly the same procedure on the second side, turning the nail outward for exactly 1¾ turns. After turning both sides, the ground fabric should be trampoline tight. Chances are that on your first try, this will not be the case, so start over and adjust and re-center the fabric by pulling on the extra fabric. This may take several tries to get right. The fabric should be centered between the shuttle poles and should be extremely tight.

Hint

Don't turn the nail more than 1¾ turns. Turning only once allows the fabric to slip, and turning more than 1¾ times will loosen the fabric when you stitch.

13. Place the nail side of the frame on a flat surface so the shuttle poles and weft bars on the nail side are on a flat surface. Make sure the shuttle poles and weft bars hit the flat surface evenly. Then gently push the top horizontal bar until it is close to the ground fabric but doesn't wrinkle the extra fabric. Turn the frame around and repeat this process with the horizontal bar. You are now ready to lace the frame.

Hint

At this point there are probably puckers along the seam lines on each side where the additional fabric is attached to the ground fabric. Don't worry, these will smooth out as the framing proceeds.

Lacing the Frame

1. For lacing, choose a very strong white cotton buttonhole and carpet twist thread and a sharp long needle. A milliners #5 or any embroidery needle will work as long as you can thread the eye and it is long enough to go through the lacing holes on the horizontal bars of the frame. I use about

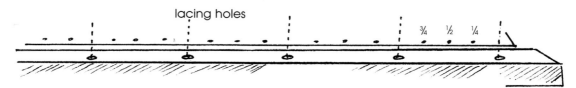

Fig. 8. Mark quarter divisions between the holes.

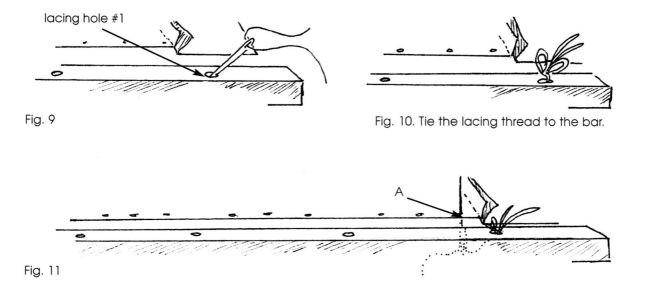

Fig. 9

Fig. 10. Tie the lacing thread to the bar.

Fig. 11

three yards of thread per side. You will cut some thread off after the lacing is complete, but starting with this length ensures that you won't run out when you start to lace across the frame.

2. Divide the distance between the lacing holes into quarters. You can make very small pencil marks on the frame to show the quarter divisions between the holes. (Fig. 8)

3. Start at the right end of the frame, with one lacing hole to the right of the seam. If there is no additional fabric, start at the last hole on the right hand side of the horizontal bar. Slant the threaded needle down through lacing hole #1. (Fig. 9)

4. Tie the lacing thread firmly to the inside of the horizontal bar. (Fig. 10)

5. Bring the needle up through the selvage of the ground fabric or on the inside of the stitch line at the first quarter mark (A) to the left of the first lacing hole where you tied the lacing thread end. (Fig. 11)

6. Take the needle down through the selvage or inside the stitched line at the third quarter mark (B), still moving toward the left. (Fig. 12)

7. The stitch length is from the first quarter mark on the horizontal bar to the third quarter mark and where the thread came up and went back down. Each of these passages should be equidistant along the selvage edge of the fabric. The stitch should be on the top of the ground fabric.

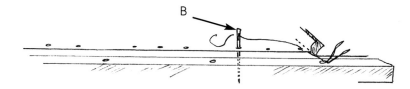

B

Fig. 12

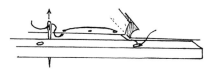

Fig. 13. Bring the needle up, needle-eye side first.

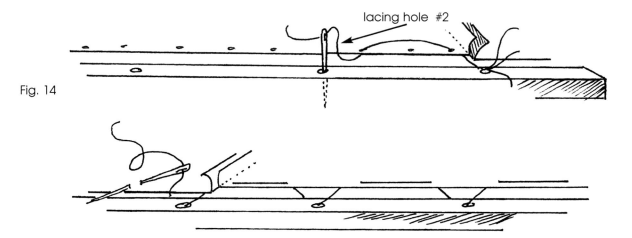

lacing hole #2

Fig. 14

Fig. 15. Stop lacing at the hole beyond the seam line.

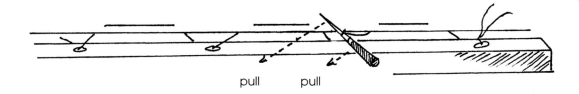

pull   pull

Fig. 16. Insert the awl under the lacing thread and pull.

8. When you complete the stitch, pass the needle up between the fabric edge and the horizontal bar, needle-eye first, so you don't puncture yourself. (Fig. 13)

9. Take the needle down through lacing hole #2 in the horizontal bar. (Fig. 14)

10. Repeat this sequence all across the fabric, stopping one lacing hole beyond the seam line or at the last lacing hole if there is no extra fabric. Leave the needle on the thread. (Fig. 15)

11. Turn the frame around and lace the second side without tightening the first side. Some people prefer to tighten the first side and then lace and tighten the second side. I have done it both ways and both work.

Tightening the Length of the Frame

1. Start on the right side of the frame. Slip an awl or laying tool under the lacing thread and pull to the left and toward yourself in a diagonal direction.

Hint

Always pull on the diagonal. If you pull the lacing thread straight down toward the bar, you will tear the fabric and break the lacing thread.

2. Pull the fabric as close to the horizontal bar as possible. (Fig. 16) Each time I remove the awl I place my thumb on the lacing thread on the horizontal bar so it doesn't slip back. The first

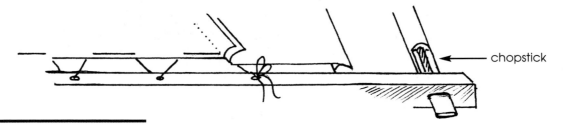

Fig. 17. Insert a chopstick piece in the cutout area.

tightening across the frame is to remove as much slack as possible. Go back and tighten a second time, then a third time to make sure it is truly tight.

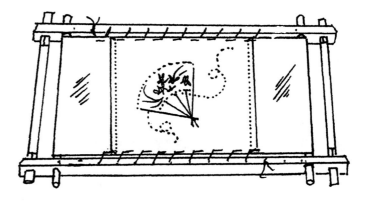

Fig. 18. The ground fabric after it's framed up.

Hint

Gradual tightening in several steps lessens the likelihood of breaking the lacing thread or making a hole in the ground fabric. If you do make a large hole in the ground fabric, place a dot of glue on the hole to prevent it from getting bigger.

3. When the fabric is tight enough, pass the lacing needle through the last hole two more times. You now have three threads in this last hole. Slip the needle under these three threads and through the loop to form a knot. Do this at least two times, then cut off the left-over lacing thread.

4. Repeat this process to tighten the second side.

Tightening the Width of the Frame

1. Turn the frame so the nail side is closest to you. Measure the cutout area of the weft bars. If the distance isn't the same, use the shortest distance.

2. Cut two pieces of chopsticks to equal this short distance. Make sure both chopstick pieces are the same length.

3. Insert a chopstick piece in the cutout area of the weft bar on the nail side of the frame. Insert the other chopstick piece in the second cutout area. Don't worry if the cutout area is a bit bigger than the chopstick piece. (Fig. 17)

4. Turn the frame around and push on the ends of the weft bars to force the frame as wide as possible. This will close the gap on the weft bar/chopstick on the other side.

5. Measure the cutout area on the weft bars on this side and use the longest length. Cut two chopstick pieces this length and insert them in the cutout areas.

Hint

If you plan to travel with your frame, tape the chopstick pieces in place.

6. The framing is complete. Any puckers along the seam line should have been smoothed when you inserted the chopsticks. The framed ground fabric should be so tight that when you push down on it, it has practically no give and pops right back. (Fig. 18)

CHAPTER 3:
TECHNIQUES FOR STITCHING GOLD WORK

Diane Horschak was named Piecework magazine's "Needleworker of the Year 2003" for "Noshi," a wonderful piece she worked on black obi silk with flat silk and real Japanese gold thread. The piece was adapted from a design from the Japanese Embroidery Center.

Couching

Since most threads used in gold work are couched, it makes sense to discuss the basics of couching. When you couch, there are two threads involved – a nonstitchable thread that lies on the surface of the work, and a much thinner thread that holds the non-stitchable thread to the surface by straddling it. Stitchable threads cans also be couched for decorative effect.

The thread that holds down the surface thread is referred to as a *couching thread*. The preferred couching thread is a very thin silk thread such as YLI Silk 100, a 100% silk thread that offers strength, durability, and shine. YLI Silk 100 comes in a fair selection of colors and can be purchased in any good fabric store. You can also use Japanese couching silk but it is more difficult to find.

If you are couching down Japanese gold or silver threads, use silk couching thread. If you are couching down a braid or twist, it is acceptable to use one strand of DMC six-strand floss. DMC is available in a much wider color selection and often when couching a braid or twist you will want to match the couching thread to the color of the surface thread. DMC six-strand floss has over 400 colors to choose from so you are very likely to find a color to match your braid.

Couching Rules

• Couch Japanese gold/silver in pairs. Couch other metallic threads singly or in pairs.

• Make couching stitches perpendicular to the thread being couched.

• Make couching stitches at equally distant intervals. On Japanese gold/silver, make the stitches at every other twist of the silver or gold, or about 3mm apart. Watch the twist on one of the two threads that comprise the pair and couch every other twist on this half pair. Remember that you are going over the whole pair, but just using the half pair to couch in even intervals. On twists and braids, the stitches should be about 1/8" apart.

• Always couch clockwise.

• Take the starting and ending threads to the back of the work with a sinking needle. See page 39 to make a sinking needle.

• When couching an outline edge, stitch all the pattern inside the outline before couching the edge (unless the directions specifically say to do otherwise).

Beginning the Couching Thread

To start a couching thread, make a very small knot in the end of the couching thread and cut off any extra tail. Place the knot on the back of your work, in the path you intend to couch. Bring the needle to the front of the fabric and back down through the ground fabric as close to the upward stitch as possible. The stitch that remains on the front of the work should be very small and is called a pinhead stitch.

Ending the Couching Thread

To end the couching thread, make two pinhead stitches underneath your stitched work, bring the thread to the top, and cut off the extra thread. People often ask me if this stitch will hold and I always tell them to make two pinhead stitches and try to pick them out. It is extremely hard to do. People also feel very uncomfortable about putting a knot on the back but this thread is so small it won't cause a lump on the front of your work.

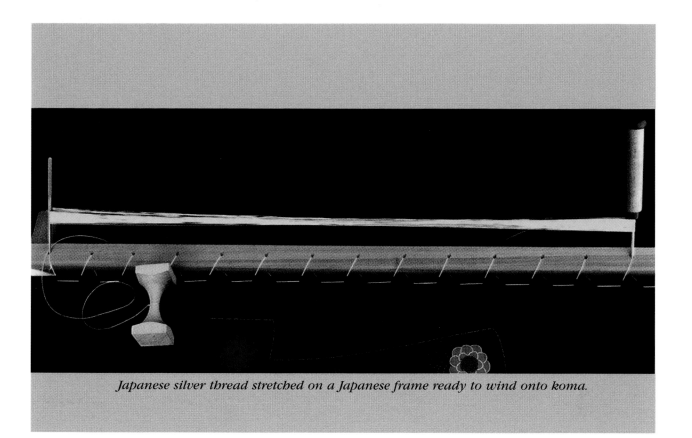

Japanese silver thread stretched on a Japanese frame ready to wind onto koma.

Winding Japanese Gold or Silver on Koma

Japanese gold or silver comes in skeins, which are usually held together by a thread or twisted with a stiff thread at one end. Open up the skein either by untwisting the stiff thread or cutting the plain thread. Set aside the stiff thread. Open the skein carefully, making sure it doesn't bunch up. The open skein will reach a length of 18" to 22". Once opened, slip the skein over the back of a chair if it will fit, or have someone hold both hands open wide in the air and place the skein over their hands, the same way you hold knitting yarn to wrap the yarn into a ball. Or place the thread around the ends of a roller frame or on a Japanese frame, place an awl in one lacing hole and a laying tool in another lacing hole far enough apart to keep the skein stretched out its full length.

Examine the skein. Instead of a loose end you may find that two ends have been tied together to make a continuous skein. If this is the case, cut it so you have two ends. Experiment to see which end comes off the skein the easiest and tangles the least. Use that end to tie and wind on the first of the two koma. Tie the single thread to one of the koma. (Fig. 1)

Place one koma in your right hand. With your left hand, unwind about 20" from the skein and place your left hand at this 20" mark. At this point your two hands should be 20" apart and the rest of the skein should still be in place. Turn the koma in your right hand toward your body, winding thread onto the koma. Whether you are right- or left-handed, always turn the koma toward your body. This adds overtwist to the Japanese gold/silver. (Fig. 2)

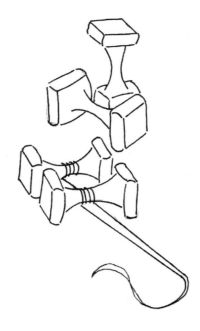

Fig. 1. Tie a thread to each of the koma.

Fig. 2. Turn the koma toward your body.

Hint

Winding the koma toward your body adds overtwist to the thread, which is very desirable. Without the overtwist, the silk core of the thread would be exposed, causing damage to the thread. As you unwind the thread from the koma, some of the overtwist will naturally disappear.

As you wind, don't let the thread slip through your left hand, as this will cause damage to the thread and leave an oily residue from your skin. Leave your left hand in the same place on the thread, letting it get closer and closer to the right hand that's holding the koma. When your two hands come together, move your left hand back another 20" and start winding again.

Wind about three yards of thread onto the first koma. Repeat the winding process on the second koma with an equal length of thread.

Retie the skein. I usually tie the skein at both ends, remove it from whatever is keeping it open, and twist it gently so it returns to its original position.

Hint

If there are kinks in the thread while you are winding it onto the koma, wind the koma away from your body until the kinks are removed. Kinks occur if there is too much overtwist on the thread. Be careful though – winding away from your body for too long will expose the silk core of the thread and will make for poor couching. Do it only until the kinks are removed.

Starting to Couch

Knot the silk couching thread and make a pinhead stitch on the line you will be covering with couching. Place a half pair (one strand) of Japanese gold/silver on the line you wish to couch, making sure you cover the starting pinhead stitch. Leave a $1/2$" tail on the surface. (This will be taken to the back of the ground fabric after couching.) Make a single couching stitch over the half pair about $1/2$" from the starting tail.

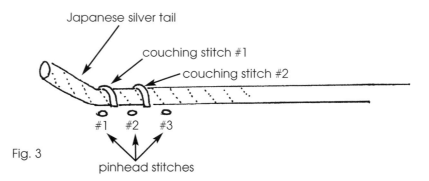

Japanese silver tail
couching stitch #1
couching stitch #2
#1 #2 #3
Fig. 3
pinhead stitches

Make another pinhead stitch with silk couching thread in the path you intend to cover with couching. This pinhead stitch will help secure the surface thread and is necessary because at this point it is very easy to pull the surface thread out from under the couching stitches.

Make a second couching stitch over the half pair, about $1/8$" (3mm) from the first couching stitch. Make a third pinhead stitch to ensure you will not pull the surface stitch out. (Fig. 3)

You are now ready to add the second half pair of Japanese gold/silver thread.

Hint

The starting end of the Japanese gold/silver remains on top of the ground fabric until later, when you sink it to the back of your work with a sinking needle. Sinking the threads to the back now would result in hanging threads on the back, which would catch in the stitching of new areas. By leaving the ends on top, you lessen the chance of catching them on the back. I prefer to sink the ends after I complete a row or section because I can then see the design areas more clearly. Some stitchers leave all the ends on top until the piece is completely finished.

Hint

For best results while couching, gently pull on the koma after each couching stitch to keep the thread taut and the couched line straight. If the thread is not couched taut, it will relax when the frame is removed and the couched line will become wavy. It is possible, but much harder, to couch metal threads without koma. If you attempt it, be sure to add overtwist to the thread while couching.

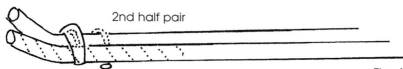

2nd half pair

Fig. 4

Hint

If you are couching a twist or braid, you probably won't add a second thread. Just continue couching from that point. It is perfectly acceptable to add a second thread later if you don't think one thread will be thick enough to cover the width of the area you want to cover. If you add another twist or braid alongside the first, don't line up the couching stitches – alternate them between the two lines of threads. This is referred to as "bricking" your stitches.

Place the second half pair next to the first half pair, leaving the same ½" of starting tail. Make a couching stitch to cover the first couching stitch and over the new half pair. This will cover up the original couching stitch and the pair of threads will have only one visible stitch over the pair of surface threads. (Fig. 4)

Make a fourth pinhead stitch to ensure the new half pair will not pull out from under the couching stitches. Make a second couching stitch over the full pair, covering the original couching stitch a second time. These two stitches cover up the first two couching stitches. You are now ready to couch around a motif or in a straight line.

Hint

Bring your needle straight up alongside the thread being couched and then straight down the other side of the thread or pair. Slanting your needle in the couching process moves the thread off the line and can pinch a pair of Japanese threads, causing an unacceptable scalloped appearance. Remember to pull on the koma after each couching stitch for an even, tight line after the piece is removed from the frame.

Couching a Square Corner

1. **Corner stitch #1**. Make the first corner stitch over the pair of threads exactly on the line you want to turn on. Make this stitch perpendicular to the pair of threads. (Fig. 5) This stitch doesn't have to be equidistant from the other stitches.

2. Before making another stitch, place the inner koma along the turning line. This makes a 90° turn. Place the outer koma straight ahead but *above the line.* (Fig. 6)

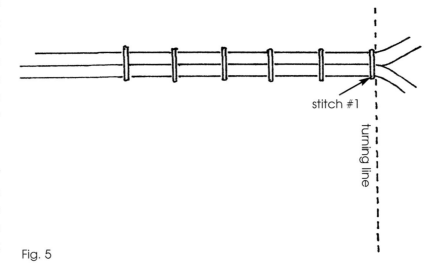

stitch #1

turning line

Fig. 5

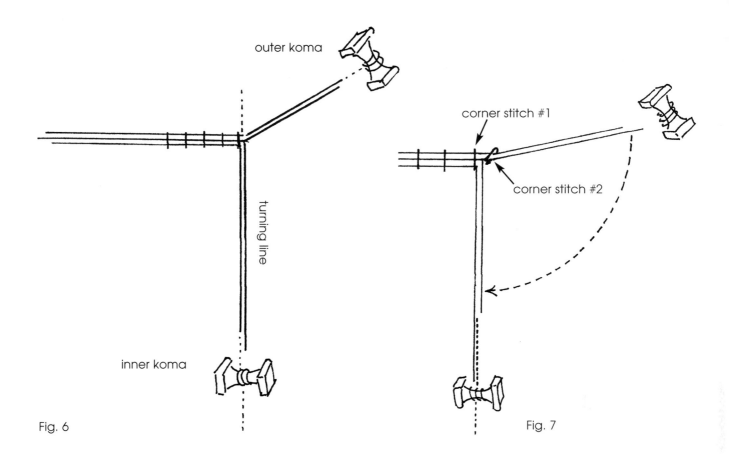

outer koma

turning line

inner koma

Fig. 6

corner stitch #1

corner stitch #2

Fig. 7

3. **Corner stitch #2**, the loop stitch. Make this stitch over the outer half pair of threads, one twist of the thread away from corner stitch #1. ***Note:*** *Make corner stitch #2 above the line of the other couching stitches.* This stitch is exaggerated so it forms a point outward. When done this way, the turn will appear very square, not rounded. Since the loop stitch is taken over a half pair of threads and is made by coming up and going down in the same hole, it compresses the thread a little to allow for a very sharp turn. (Fig. 7)

4. After making corner stitch #2, hold the couching thread taut and pull the outer koma so it runs parallel with the inner koma.

5. **Corner stitch #3.** Bring the needle to the top of the ground fabric, sharing the hole with the first stitch (#2 on the diagram). Make a perpendicular couching stitch over the pair of threads. (Fig. 8)

Hint

Stitches #1 and #3 should be an equal distance from stitch #2 and form a 90° angle.

6. When you view the completed three stitches, you will see a small space between the threads where the ground fabric is exposed. If you have more than one corner in a design, this opening should be the same size in all corners.

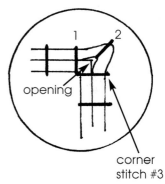

opening

corner stitch #3

Fig. 8

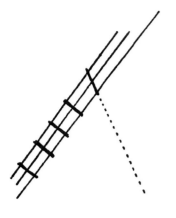
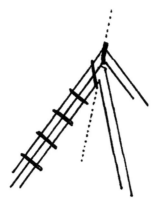
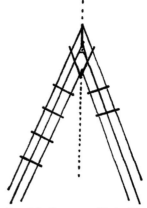

Fig. 9. Corner stitch #1 on the diagonal.

Fig. 10. Corner stitch #2.

Fig. 11. Corner stitch #3.

Couching a Sharp Corner

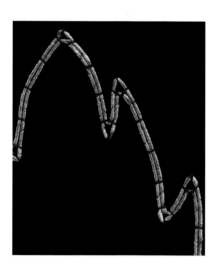

Use the same three stitches as for the square corner, but with slight adjustments.

1. **Corner stitch #1.** Take this stitch on the turning line, but not perpendicular to the metal thread pair. Make this stitch to follow the diagonal line of the turn. (Fig. 9)

2. Make **corner stitch #2** over a half pair and one twist of the thread away from stitch #1, as you did for the square corner. (Fig. 10)

3. Make **corner stitch #3** over the full pair, just as you did for the square turn, but angle it to match stitch #1. Stitch #1 and stitch #3 still share a hole at the turn. (Fig. 11)

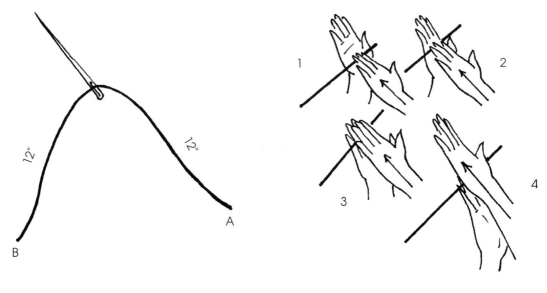

Fig. 12

Fig. 13

Making a Sinking Needle to End Couching

1. Select one or two strands of silk or cotton and thread them into a sharp #24 chenille needle. If you are sinking the ends of Japanese gold/silver, it is important that the diameter of the needle be big enough to create a hole in the fabric that will allow the metal thread to slip through without stripping the paper off the core.

2. Double the thread so the needle is in the center of the length. The diagram shows 12" on each side of the needle, which is a workable length. (Fig. 12)

3. Securely anchor the needle to the ground fabric so your hands are free. Place thread end A in your mouth and hold it tight.

4. Place thread end B at the base of the palm of your right hand (the needle is still in the middle of the thread and securely held in place). Hold thread end B in place with the fingertips of your left hand.

Roll thread end B with your left fingertips up your right palm. Roll the length of your two hands. The thread will end in the palm of your left hand. (Fig. 13)

5. Repeat the process a second time and a third if necessary. This is referred to as *undertwisting* thread end B.

6. Place the twisted thread end B in your mouth and repeat the process with thread end A.

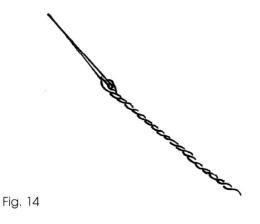

Fig. 14

Fig. 15

7. When the undertwisting is complete, put both twisted threads together at the base of your left palm and with the fingertips of your right hand, roll up your left hand. Repeat. This process adds overtwist to the thread. The result is a twisted thread with the needle caught in the middle. (Fig. 14)

8. Thread the twisted thread back through the needle's eye to form a loop. (Fig. 15)

Sinking the Ends

Sink all the thread ends to the back of your work using a sinking needle.

1. Cut the metal thread ends to a length of ½" or a little shorter.

2. Insert the sinking needle in the top of the ground fabric at the precise point where you want to take the metal thread to the back of the work.

Hint

Examine the thread ends before you sink them and visualize how the thread endings will look after they have been sunk. Once you sink a thread, it is very hard to pull it back to the top and move it over a bit.

3. Take the sinking needle to the back of the ground fabric, leaving the loop on top of the fabric.

4. Place the loop around the metal thread end, leaving a little slack in the metal thread. Make a quick downward motion on the needle and pull the loop through to the back of the work. The loop will automatically close like a noose and neatly "pop" the metal thread to the back.

Hint

Always sink a half pair at a time and always sink each half pair in separate holes in the ground fabric.

5. Turn your work to the back. Use couching thread to bend the metal threads over and whipstitch them to the back of your work.

6. Run the needle through a loop of thread to make a small knot and cut off the end.

Transferring Designs to Fabric

There are many transfer pencils and transfer papers available, but I prefer to transfer designs to the ground fabric with stitches – running backstitches to be exact. I have tried many other transferring methods and I prefer this one. With a stitched line, it's easy to remove a mistake without leaving a mark on the ground fabric. Simply remove the incorrect stitches and restitch the line. This is especially beneficial when working on very costly ground fabric such as obi silk.

Another reason I like this method is that stitching the transfer lines familiarizes you with each design line. Especially when couching a curved line, it is important that the line curve beautifully, with no hitch in the continuous curve. If you have already stitched that curved line with a running stitch, you have educated your eye to know exactly how the curve turns. So this method serves two purposes – getting your design on the fabric and familiarizing yourself with the design.

I learned a very important concept while studying in Japan – "It is a very long way from your mind to your finger-tips." It is very easy to learn an embroidery concept in your mind but it is another thing to stitch it perfectly. Transferring by stitching may take extra time, but it will prove very valuable in the end result.

Transferring with Stitching

1. Trace the pattern onto paper. Tracing paper and tissue paper work equally well. Use a permanent marker, not a pencil, to do the tracing. Pencil can rub off on the stitching thread and soil the ground fabric. If your design is on plain paper, you can buy tracing paper sturdy enough to be used in a copy machine and copy the design onto the tracing paper to eliminate the tracing handwork.

2. After you've traced the design, place the paper on the ground fabric with the *unmarked side facing the ground fabric*. The marked side should never touch the fabric.

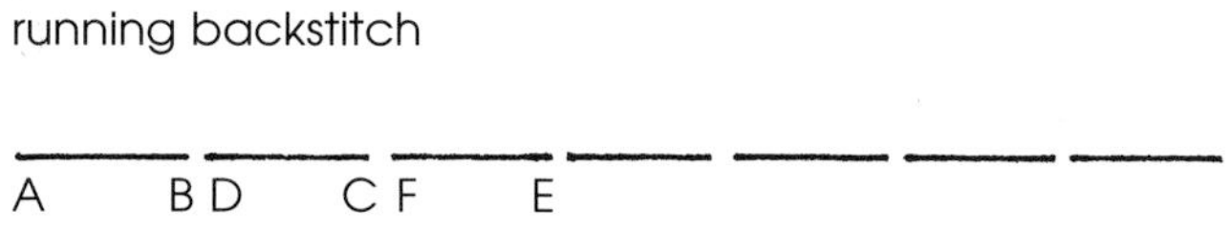

running backstitch

———— —— —— —————— ———— ——————
A   B D   C F   E

Fig. 17

3. Baste the paper tracing to the ground fabric or use magnets to hold it in place. If you plan to baste around the outer edge of the design, first test your ground fabric to make sure you won't make permanent holes in the fabric. I prefer to place a magnet at each corner. You can purchase small magnets at needlework stores that won't leave a residue on the ground fabric.

4. Use couching thread and a #9 crewel needle to stitch running backstitches through every design line. The size of the stitches should not exceed ⅛" (3mm). (Fig. 16 and 17)

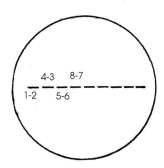

Fig. 16. Actual size of running backstitches – ⅛" (3mm).

5. As you stitch the running backstitches, pull the stitches reasonably tight so that when you later pull the paper tracing away, the stitches will not loosen. Make sure your stitches accurately follow the traced lines. These are the lines you will follow when stitching the design and the more accurate they are, the easier it will be to stitch.

6. When you've completed the outline stitching, tear the paper away to reveal the stitched outline of the design. This sounds easy, but you must be very careful not to disturb the stitching when tearing away the paper. I usually run the point of a laying tool along a single stitched line. Since the paper has already been perforated by the running backstitches, this further breaks the perforation and makes tearing easier. Carefully tear away that portion of the paper and move to another stitched line. It is helpful to have a pair of small tweezers to remove the tiny bits of paper left on the fabric.

7. Check the stitched design to see if every line is correct. Compare it to the original design and make sure you transferred it exactly. Make adjustments if necessary. Keep the original drawing handy as a reference while stitching.

Transferring with Transfer Paper

1. Place the paper, transfer-side-down, on the ground fabric and secure it with magnets on the four corners. Be sure to place the magnets outside the design area, in case they leave a smudge.

2. Lay the design on top of the transfer paper and use a sharp pencil or transfer stylus to trace the lines of the design. Be very careful not to shift the paper or the design while tracing and don't handle or put too much weight on the transfer paper or it will leave a smudge on the fabric.

CHAPTER 4:
GOLD WORK DOVE – A BEGINNING PROJECT

For illustrative purposes, the silver thread in this project is couched with red-orange couching thread. This is not a usual practice, but the red-orange thread allows you to see the couching stitches, which would have been much harder if done in the traditional white or pale blue on silver.

Fig. 1. Pattern for Gold Work Dove.

You Will Need

• 10" x 10" piece of firm ground fabric, preferably a tightly woven silk
Note: *If you have difficulty finding a fine grade of silk fabric, try an independent fabric store. The fabric must be firm enough to support the gold/silver threads. Look for a very tightly woven silk substantial in feel. The silk used as lining material is much too thin for this work. I don't usually buy blends like polyester and cotton because they can stretch and won't support the gold/silver couching to its best advantage. However, if that's all you can find, try a small piece. It should be fine for this project because you will be couching single rows of silver. A very good piece of cotton should also work.*

• Frame – either a Japanese frame or roller frame
• Pair of koma
• Needles:
    couching needle – #9 or #10 crewel needle or #2 or #3
        machine-made Japanese needle
    #24 chenille needle
    sinking needle (see page 39)
• Laying tool
• Thread:
    Japanese silver or gold, size 5
    silk couching thread – YLI Silk 100, pale blue or white for
        silver, red or gold for gold
    lacing thread – Coats and Clark Button Craft Dual Duty thread
        (called carpet and buttonhole twist)
    7" to 12" silver check purl (sometimes called frieze purl)
• Tracing or tissue paper

Preparing to Stitch

1. Frame up the ground fabric. Refer to the framing instructions in Chapter 2.

2. Transfer the dove design (Fig. 1) to the ground fabric. Follow the instructions on page 41 to transfer the dove pattern onto tracing or tissue paper, then onto the ground fabric. If you are transferring the design by stitching the outline, thread a #9 crewel needle with couching thread to do the running backstitches. The ground fabric in this project is blue and the thread being couched is silver, so I used white silk couching thread for the transfer running backstitches.

3. The design size is 4". If you plan to make an ornament as shown, place the design tracing on half of the fabric and save the other half for the back. If you plan to frame the piece rather than make an ornament, center the design on the fabric.

4. Wind the Japanese silver onto two koma (see page 34 for instructions). Always have the silver thread come off the koma from the bottom. For best results while couching, pull gently on the koma after each couching stitch to keep the silver taut and the couched line straight. If the silver thread is not couched taut, it will relax when the frame is removed and the couched line will become wavy. It is possible, but much harder, to couch metal threads without koma. If you do, be sure to add overtwist to the thread while couching.

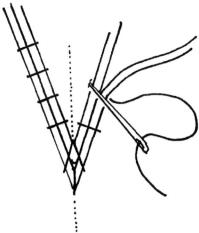

Fig. 2. Make the corner, then continue couching.

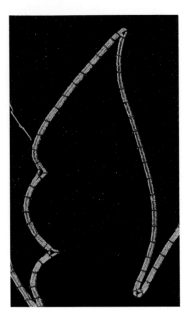

Beginning to Couch the Dove Outline

1. Working clockwise, couch a pair of #5 Japanese silver starting at the dove's beak and working down the head.

Hint

Bring your needle straight up alongside the silver, then straight down the other side of the thread pair. If you slant your needle in the couching process, you will move the silver thread off the line and may also pinch the silver, causing a scalloped appearance. Remember to pull on the koma after each couching stitch to secure an even, light line after the piece is removed from the frame.

2. When you reach the end of the neck you will need to couch a sharp corner before continuing to couch up the outer wing. Whether you are turning a square corner or a pointed corner like this one, the first stitch is always over the pair of threads at the line to turn. (Fig. 2)

3. Continue couching up the wing of the dove until you reach the tip of the wing where you will again turn a sharp corner.

4. While couching down the side of the wing, you will make a series of small sharp corners to form the fluted edge of the wing. (Fig. 3)

5. Continue couching with one pair of Japanese silver around the outside of the dove until you reach the starting point on the beak.

6. When you reach the beak, cut both metal threads ½" beyond the last couching stitch. You now have four tails in this area – two from the start of couching and two from the end.

7. End your couching thread by making two pinhead stitches under the couched line. Then bring your couching thread to the front and cut off the thread.

8. Sink all the thread ends to the back of your work (see page 40 for instructions).

9. Couch the second pair around the body next to the first pair.

Couching the Branch

1. Couch the branch in the dove's mouth with a half pair of Japanese silver, starting and stopping as you did for the dove's body.

2. Cut and sink the thread ends.

3. Cut six or seven ¼" long pieces of check purl to embellish the branch.

Hint

When cutting check purl, lay the uncut pieces on a piece of felt to keep them from "jumping" around.

4. To attach the check purl pieces to the ground fabric, slip a threaded #9 crewel needle through the hollow core and sew the pieces to the ground fabric just like you would attach a bead.

Couching the Back Wing

1. Couch a pair of Japanese silver to couch around the back wing of the dove, starting and stopping as you did for the dove's body.

2. Cut and sink the thread ends.

3. There are two pair couched on the front body and one pair around the back wing.

Finishing

1. Before removing the stitched piece from the frame, sink and secure all the metal thread ends. On the back of the piece, secure the ends with whipstitches.

2. To make an ornament, mark a 4" circle around the couched design, leaving ½" around the dove. Cut out the circle, then cut another circle the same size from the ground fabric for the back.

3. With wrong sides together, slipstitch the two circles together with invisible thread. Stuff with polyester.

4. Hide the slipstitches by embellishing the edge with a cord or twisted thread. This also gives a finished look.

5. Stitch a bow hanger on the top of the finished piece.

CHAPTER 5:
"GOLDEN LEAVES" – A PALETTE FOR GOLD WORK TECHNIQUES

During one of my study trips to Japan, I bought a roll of Ra ground fabric with five different leaf patterns woven into the fabric. I had no idea what I would do with the fabric – I just thought it was wonderful and had to have it. I knew it would talk to me one day and out would come an idea to embellish the leaves. As I looked at the leaves and their wonderfully shaped edges, they seemed the perfect palette to embellish with many varieties of gold work and redefine the edges with couched gold thread. The bank fabric that is left unstitched adds richness to the gold work and a shadow effect to the leaves.

All the techniques used in "Golden Leaves" can be done on the ground fabric of your choice. Any good quality silk fabric will work. Look for silk fabric of substantial weight. Any color of silk will work and the finish can be shiny or matte. Lightweight lining silks will not work, nor will linen or cotton fabrics because they are not heavy enough to support the gold threads.

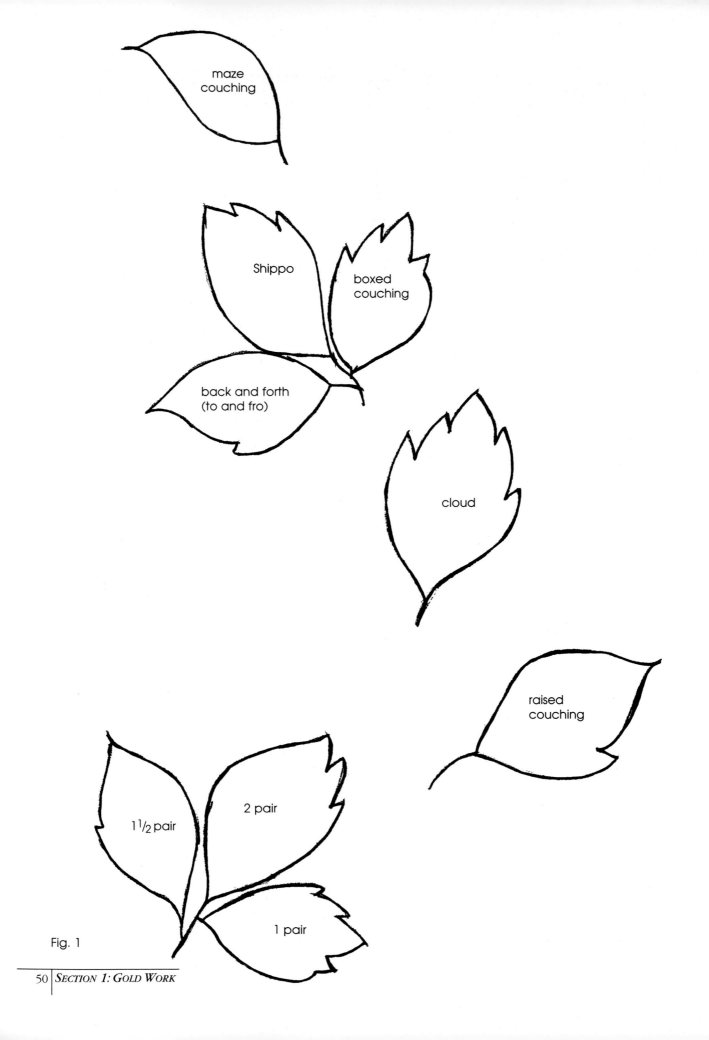

maze
couching

Shippo

boxed
couching

back and forth
(to and fro)

cloud

raised
couching

1 1/2 pair

2 pair

1 pair

Fig. 1

Examples of the leaves in progress. In this example, the leaves are couched with Japanese gold and red couching thread on black obi silk.

Use the pattern of three leaves (Fig. 1) to practice the gold work techniques that follow. Transfer the pattern onto a substantial silk ground fabric with running backstitches and experiment with the various ways of doing gold work.

Start with a simple exercise – couching three different edges on a cluster of three leaves.

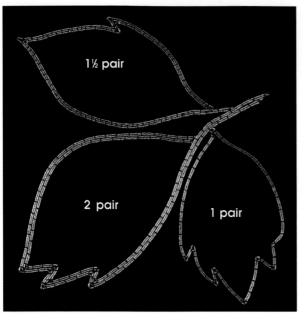

Fig. 2

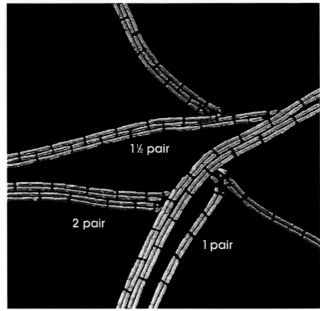

Fig. 3

Couched Japanese gold makes wonderful edges. Edges can be stitched in various thicknesses as pictured here - a single pair, a pair and a half, and two pair.

Couching the Edges

The basic technique of couching an edge provides a frame for open stitching patterns or motifs and gives a finished appearance to the design. The couched edge acts much like the frame around a painting – it stops your eye from running off the edge of the picture. However, the frame should not be so elaborate that it is the first and only thing you see. Japanese gold/silver makes a suitable frame that stops the eye without interfering with the pattern.

Couching stitches on Japanese gold are made with red-orange couching thread, which is believed to enhance and enrich the gold color.

It is important to maintain an equal distance between couching stitches. The accepted interval is every other twist of the gold. Choose one of the pair of gold threads to watch for marking the twists. The twists on a pair of gold do not have to line up. The interval rule is amended somewhat when reaching a tip or going around a very tight curve. In those instances, the stitches are slightly closer together.

Hint

The couched edge should be smooth, with no dips in the line, and the curve should curve perfectly. Use koma to hold the Japanese gold in place and move the koma slightly at the end of every stitch to conform to the curve. Tug on the koma after each stitch to maintain a constant tension on the gold, which will result in straight rows. Without proper tension on the gold, when the piece is unframed the line of gold will relax and become wobbly.

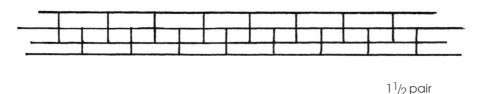

Fig. 4   1¹/₂ pair

Fig. 5   2 pair

Couching an Edge with One Pair

Refer to the Dove project on page 46 to couch the outline of the leaf clockwise. When couching one pair around a motif such as these leaves, the tips require a sharp turn so refer to the instructions for turning a sharp corner on page 38. Sink all the ends.

Couching an Edge with a Pair and a Half

Using a pair and a half instead of one pair will create a slightly stronger edge. Start by couching one pair clockwise around the motif. Sink all the ends.

Again couching clockwise, start the second row with one koma (half pair) placed at the outer edge of the original pair. Pass the couching thread over the new half pair and over the outside half pair of the first couched row. This makes the stitch over a full pair. Place the stitch between the stitches of the first row. This process is called "bricking." (Fig. 4)

Hint

In bricking, the second row of couching stitches falls exactly between the first row of couching stitches. When couching subsequent rows, the third row lines up with the first row. The fourth row of couching stitches lines up with the second row, and so on.

Couching an Edge with Two Pair

An open pattern in the center of a motif might require a stronger edge, in which case you would couch the edge with two pair of Japanese gold.

To couch two pair, couch the first pair completely around and sink the ends. Then couch a second pair on the outside of the first pair. Brick the second pair to the first pair. (Fig. 5)

It is acceptable to couch multiple rows if you need a wider edge.

Fig. 6. Shippo couching pattern. The sides of the green squares are 1cm.

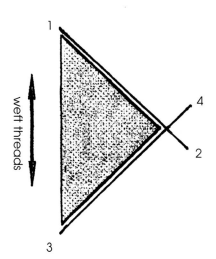

Fig. 7

Shippo

The lattice lines shown under the Shippo shapes are temporary and will be pulled out after the shapes are all couched.

Shippo Couching

The curving lines of Shippo couching form a very pleasing pattern. This is a traditional pattern found on all types of decorations in Japan. There is not a standard size for Shippo, so it is acceptable to vary the size of the shapes as desired.

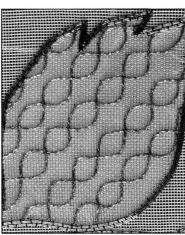

Fig. 8

1. Before couching, set up temporary guidelines within the leaf, using the pattern in the illustration. Make a knot in the end of one strand of gold couching thread. Place the knot on the back of the work. Bring the couching thread to the top of work at an edge of the leaf and use a 45° triangle to lay a stitch along each edge of the triangle. (Fig. 7)

2. Stitch parallel lines in both directions exactly 1cm apart. This will form a stitched lattice. When the lattice stitching is completed, end the couching thread by making two pinhead stitches close to an intersection.

3. With one strand of gold couching thread, couch the lattice at the intersections only (the green lines on the chart). You will leave the couching stitches and pinhead stitches in the ground fabric, but you will remove the lattice threads after you've couched the Shippo shapes.

4. Wind one half pair of size 4 or 5 Japanese gold on a koma.

5. Place the first couching stitch (1-2) at the intersection of the temporary holding thread close to the edge of the leaf (A). Don't start in the center of the leaf because you are going to couch the line from

one side of the leaf to the other. It takes two journeys to complete one full line of Shippo. Start on the edge and follow the red line on the chart. This is the first journey across. Note the couching stitches on the chart. Once you've couched this line across the entire leaf it will be couched back in a return journey.

6. Place the second couching stitch in the center of the curve, the width of the serpentine shape. Measure the distance from the center couching stitch to the lattice line. All the center couching stitches should be the same distance

from the center latticed couched line on both journeys. This distance can vary from 2mm to 4mm depending on the desired size. It is important to maintain the same width throughout the area. This is true with the red line couched across and the blue line couched on the return journey. (Fig. 8)

7. Place the third couching stitch halfway between the center couching stitch and the starting stitch (4-5 on Fig. 8).

8. Place the fourth couching stitch halfway between the center and the next intersection of the temporary holding threads (6-7 on Fig. 8).

9. Make the next couching stitch at the intersection of the lattice threads.

10. Continue until you reach the end of the leaf. Turn the thread and couch back along the blue line, forming the serpentine shape on the other side of the temporary holding thread. Be sure to measure the distance from the center stitch

to the lattice thread. Each side of the Shippo should be equal.

11. When you reach the end of this first Shippo row, sink the ends of the gold thread and start a new row. If you used a braid, take the braid to the back of the work with a chenille needle and bring it to the top to make a second row.

12. When you've completed all the rows of the Shippo couching in both diagonal directions, carefully pull out the gold lattice couching thread lines. The gold couching stitches, which are now hidden, will remain.

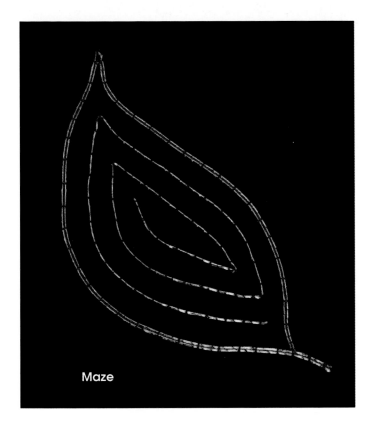

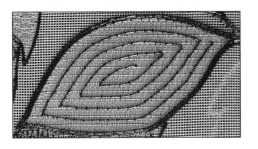

Maze couching with a full pair of Japanese gold couched around the outside of the motif. After that, the inside rows were couched with a half pair of Japanese gold.

Maze Couching

Normally when stitching a motif such as the leaves, you would stitch the inside pattern first, then the edge. In the case of maze couching, you couch the outside edge first because you will measure the inside maze pattern off the edge line. Traditionally the edge is couched with one pair of Japanese gold and the maze pattern (Fig. 9 on page 58) is couched with a half pair of Japanese gold. The thread used to do maze couching can be one size smaller than the thread used on the edge, so if you couched size 4 Japanese gold around the edge, you could use size 3 Japanese gold for the maze pattern inside the leaf.

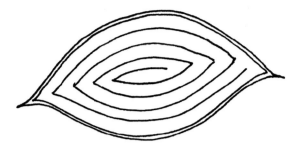

Fig. 9. Maze couching pattern.

1. Couch one pair of Japanese gold (size 3 to 5) around the outer edge of the leaf. Measure the maze stitches off this first row of couching.

2. After you've couched the outside pair, cut and sink the thread ends.

3. With a half pair of gold (usually one size smaller than the edge), start the maze couching at the base of the leaf. To find the starting place, measure a point exactly 3mm inside the outline and make the first couching stitch over the half pair. Continuing clockwise up the side of the leaf, measure each stitch and make sure the distance between the first pair and the half pair is exactly 3mm.

Hint

I measure from the center or inside of the first pair, then bring the needle up on the 3mm mark on my ruler and go over the half pair of gold. This ensures that the distance between the rows is exactly 3mm.

4. After couching a short distance up the first edge, sink the starting Japanese gold thread. Usually you would leave the tail on top of the work and sink it later, but in this case when you come down the other edge to start the next row, having the tail on top would make it hard to measure the new row. Take the tail to the back to get it out of the way.

5. Couch clockwise up the leaf, maintaining exactly 3mm between the two lines. (If you were couching a larger area, the space between the lines could be 4mm or 5mm.)

6. Turn at the tip of the leaf and couch down the other side of the leaf. Maintain the 3mm interval between the outside full pair and the inside half pair.

7. At the bottom, turn and couch up the inside, maintaining the 3mm interval. End in the center of the leaf and make the last row of couching 3mm from both sides.

8. Sink the half pair and end the couching thread with two pinhead stitches.

If you don't think one pair around the edge is strong enough to set off the maze couching, return to the outside and couch one more pair of Japanese gold around the edge, giving you an outer edge two pair wide. I prefer to add this second row of couching around the outside after the maze is complete, which makes measuring off the first pair easier.

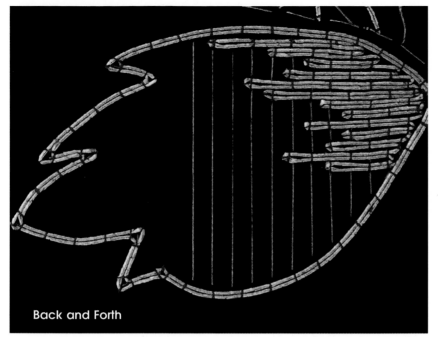

Back and Forth

The vertical lines are temporary and will be removed after the couching is finished. These temporary lines are stitched with YLI 100 silk thread.

Back and Forth Couching

This technique, also called "to and fro" couching, has one thing in common with maze couching – the outside edge is always couched before the interior. Maze and back and forth couching are the only two techniques where this is true. Back and forth is unique in that a complete row is made of two journeys – an outward and an inward – done with a half pair each.

1. Couch one pair of gold threads around the outside edge.

Hint

When couching this technique on canvas, stitched guidelines aren't necessary because the rows of holes serve as guidelines.

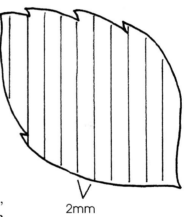

Fig. 10. Space the guidelines 2mm apart.

2mm

2. With gold couching thread, lay parallel guidelines 2mm apart inside the leaf. (Fig. 10) If your motif is large, the guidelines may be 3mm or 4mm apart or if it's small, they could be 1mm apart. The lines act as couching guides to place and keep the couching stitches in straight rows. Some of the guidelines will be completely covered and not removed; others will be cut out and removed when all the couching has been completed.

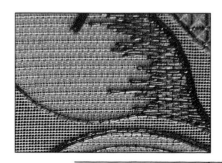

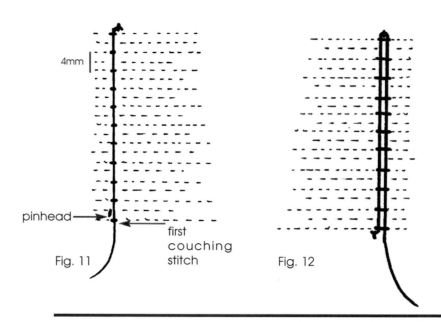

4mm

pinhead ——►

first
couching
stitch

Fig. 11   Fig. 12

3. Start at a couched edge, stitching the outward journey first. Place one koma with a half pair on the couched edge of the motif. Make a couching stitch close to the couched outline over the half pair, then a pinhead stitch.

4. Couch outward from the starting edge on *every other* guideline, making the couching stitches 4mm apart. When you reach the point farthest from the edge, make a couching stitch even if it is not in the interval pattern. Make a pinhead stitch and turn the gold thread to come back parallel to the first couched row. (Fig. 11)

Hint

Couching the outward journey is only done on the first row. Every outward journey from this point on will not be couched on the outward journey. This first row is done to stabilize the next rows.

5. Stitch the inward journey next. Make a couching stitch over the pair of gold, close to the turn, then couch over the pair of threads on the return journey, *covering the previous couching stitches*. Every inward journey after the first will have couching stitches over the full pair of gold. You are now at the starting edge of the leaf. Turn the gold and take a couching stitch close to the couched outer edge to prepare to start the second row. (Fig. 12)

Hint

In back and forth couching, the completion of the outward and inward journey equals one row.

6. Make the turning stitch and start the second row at the edge. Make the first couching stitch as close to the outer couched line as possible and make the next couching stitch at the outer edge of the outward journey. (Fig. 13)

Hint

Because there is a couching stitch at the beginning and end of this first journey and no couching stitches between, pull the koma to make sure this line is straight and firm.

7. Make a pinhead stitch at the outer edge. Turn the metallic thread by pulling the koma toward the starting edge. Take a stitch close to the turn over the full pair. If the metallic thread doesn't turn easily or twists, there could be too much overtwist on the metallic. Turn the koma away from your body about 10 turns before pulling the metallic for the return journey. This will remove some of the overtwist on the metallic and make it easier to turn.

8. Couch back over the full pair on every other guideline and brick the stitches to the first couched row. (Fig. 14)

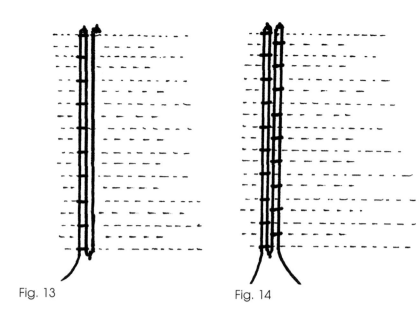

Fig. 13 Fig. 14

9. At this point the gold is back at the edge of the leaf, ready to be turned for the third outward journey. Turn the gold outward and make a couching stitch, then a pinhead stitch to prevent it from coming loose. Carry the gold to the outermost limit and couch, make a pinhead stitch, and turn for the return journey.

Hint

Except on the first row, all outward journeys are couched over the half pair at the beginning and end of the journey. The inward journey is couched over the full pair of threads, with every other row bricked to the adjacent row.

10. Stop the outer edges in a random fashion to create a fading effect, which adds to the beauty of back and forth couching. The fading technique is very apparent behind the green flower in the photo below.

Notice the fading technique in the back and forth background stitching.

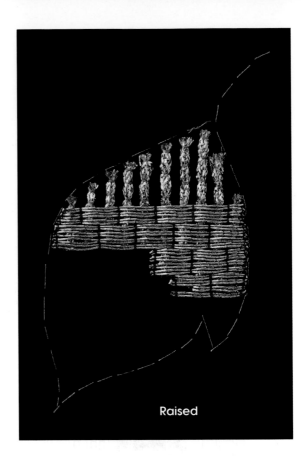

In raised couching, the thick vertical lines are the padding stitches and the horizontal couched rows flow over the padding threads. Note that the padding threads end on top of the work and are not taken to the back of the work.

Raised

Raised Couching

Raised couching is also called padded couching and basket stitch filling. In this technique you couch a metallic thread or Japanese gold over padding threads to form hills and valleys. This is a wonderful technique for filling in an area and can create a very dramatic effect.

Historically, string was couched perpendicular to the rows of gold with small stitches approximately every $1/4"$. The close stitches were made by coming up on the outside of the string, then piercing the string in the middle to make the downward stitch. The stitches alternated coming up at the top or bottom of the string. All the stitches pierced the string and the string was cut to fit the exact row length.

Today, padding threads are usually #16 or #32 braid in a color that matches the thread used to make the raised couching pattern. The braid can be stitched in even intervals on canvas or couched an equal distance apart on fabric. Couch the braid the same way as the string, alternating the couching stitches on each side of the braid. Gold braid is an excellent choice because if the top couching exposes the padding the least bit, the gold color will blend with the couching. Braid is also firm enough to form the hills and doesn't ravel when the ends are cut. (Fig. 15)

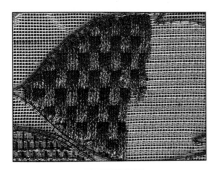

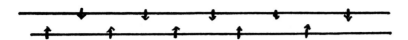

Fig. 15. Alternate stitches on each side of the padding thread.

Fig. 16. Raised couching pattern on canvas. The black lines are padding.

There are many patterns used for this couching method. If you are doing this technique on canvas, lay the padding every four to eight holes apart, choose your intervals, and remain consistent. (Fig. 16)

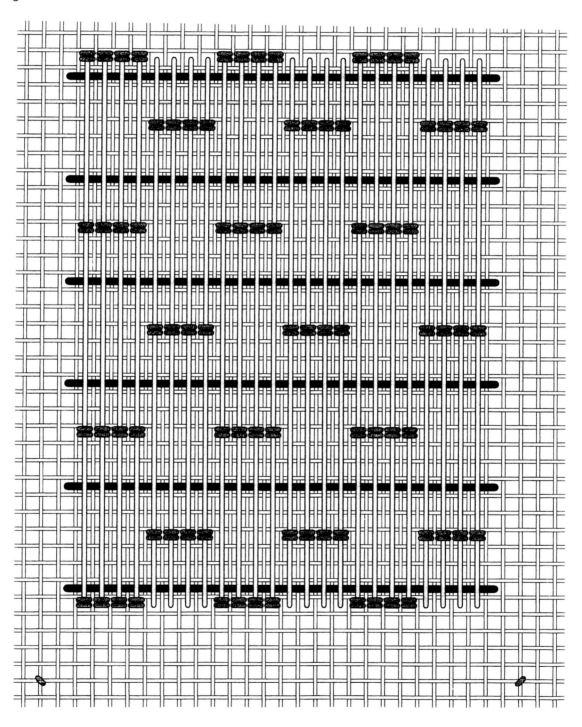

The black lines in the chart are the padding threads, shown on canvas. Note that the couching stitches on the padding threads don't show because they are covered up by the light gray couched lines.

Hint

It is easy to couch at even intervals on canvas. On fabric you must be very careful to make the couching rows line up.

1. Lay the padding (braid) over the whole motif area. Carefully measure each row from the previous row and make sure the rows are an equal distance apart. End the padding thread and couch it in place.

2. Start the first row of gold at the left bottom edge of the motif. Lay the thread to be couched perpendicular to the padding (light gray on the chart).

Hint

If you are making a garment or a piece that will have heavy wear, wax the couching thread before using it. If the end product will be a picture, it is not necessary to wax the thread because the wax can attract dust and the double couching stitch is strong enough to hold the metallic.

3. Thread a needle with couching thread, place the knot in the back of the ground fabric, and make a pinhead stitch. Make the first couching stitch by bringing the needle up on the right side of the gold and taking it down on the left side, making sure your needle comes up straight and goes down straight (a slanted needle can move the gold and make for uneven rows or cause the couching stitch to pinch the metallic).

4. Make a second couching stitch on top of the first couching stitch.

5. Repeat the couching process with the gold metallic traveling over *two* padding threads. From this point to the end of the row, couch every two padding threads. Make the couching stitch in the center of the two padding stitches to form the valley. As the metallic flows over the padding, it forms the hill.

Hint

Don't pull the gold metallic too tight or you'll flatten the hills and valleys.

6. When you've completed the length of the row, on canvas or counted ground fabric, take the metallic to the back and come up in the next row of holes. When couching with Japanese gold, you can either cut the gold and sink the ends or you can turn the pair of threads and couch back. If you cut the threads, sink the ends later. The second row of couching stitches should line up with the first row.

7. Couch two more rows of gold, matching up the couching stitches.

8. On the fifth row of couching, brick the couching stitches to the first set of stitches. Continue for three more rows. The ninth row of couching stitches should line up with the first four rows of couching.

Hint

The number of rows that line up can vary but you always take two couching stitches, one on top of the other.

The possibilities in raised couching are endless. The top couching pattern can be varied, as can the height and width of the padding. The padding spacing or the length of the rows of padding can vary. The area being filled can start with the metallic couched flat at either end and then gradually be padded approaching the center area. Some of the string can be left uncovered and covered later with satin stitches of another thread or metallic. The metallic threads can also vary. I have couched rows of gold, then alternated with rows of silver or rows of silk. If you alternate rows of silver with rows of white silk or white metallic, the light that plays off the different heights of metallic adds to the beauty.

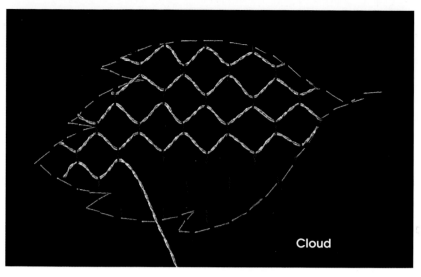

Cloud

In cloud filling, the stitches are an equal distance apart and the gold is couched on the surface.

Cloud Filling

Cloud filling is in the family of open filling stitches. These surface stitches lend texture and pattern to an area with an open pattern in gold threads. They are decorative patterns laid in a repetitive pattern, allowing the background fabric to shadow through. The couching thread is often decorative or a contrasting color to the metal thread.

This particular stitch could also be categorized as surface weaving because you lay a series of small stitches in a repeat pattern, then weave the metal thread in and out of the small stitches. These decorative repeat filling stitches create an open, airy effect that is often a great complement to a solidly filled gold area.

1.Refer to the pattern on page 66 (Fig. 17). Thread a #9 crewel needle with couching thread. Knot the thread and place the knot on the back of the work. Make a pinhead stitch in an area that you know will be covered with stitches.

2. Make couching stitches at precise even intervals. On canvas the stitches are eight threads apart and two threads wide. The second row is bricked to the first row. From that point, the odd row couching stitches line up with each other and the even row couching stitches line up with each other. On fabric the couching stitches are 2mm to 3mm wide and approximately 8mm to 10mm apart. There is a width of 8mm to 10mm from Row #1 to Row #3, with Row #2 being bricked in between.

3.After you've done the couching stitches, make two pinhead stitches and bring the couching thread to the surface and cut it off.

4.Thread the metallic thread in a large-eyed needle such as a size 22 tapestry needle. Start at the leaf's edge and thread under each couching stitch only on the surface of the ground fabric. Note the undulating pattern that encompasses two rows of couching stitches. You can use braids, twist, and most metal threads to thread through couching stitches.

5. After completing the first row, take the thread to the back of the work and come up very close to the downward stitch. Thread back up the leaf, sharing the couching stitches on one side of the journey.

6. Continue until all the rows are complete. Make sure the metallic stays on the surface of the ground fabric and is taken to the back only at the end of each row.

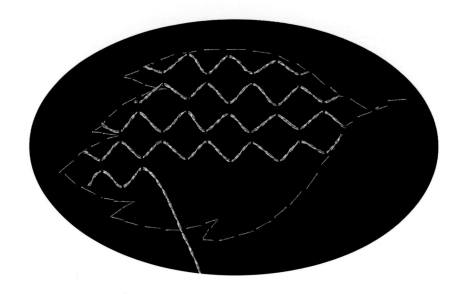

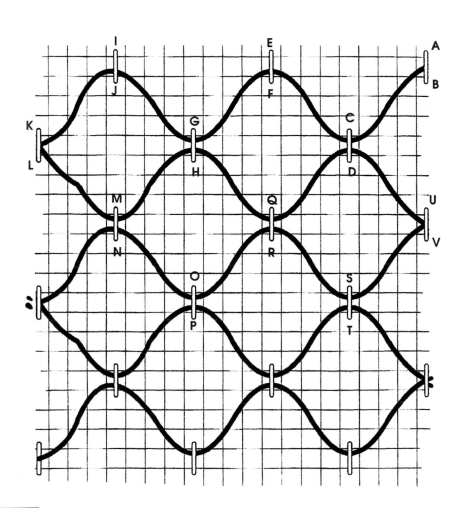

Fig. 17

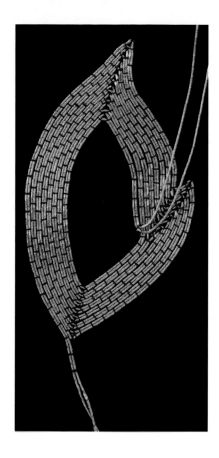

The pattern at the corners is created by turning the gold.

Boxed Couching

Boxed couching is used to fill an area completely in Japanese gold or silver. In Oriental embroidery, you couch around the outside line, then place each subsequent row inside the starting row, couching round and round to fill the area completely. The rows of Japanese gold or silver are bricked, and as you approach the center, there may be room for a half pair of gold. If so, sink a half pair and proceed couching the other half pair to fill the center of the motif.

Think about the shape to be filled. Fill an irregular shape around the edge first. As you approach the center, it could narrow into different areas to fill completely. This is fine and the movement of the gold gives wonderful light play with even more reflection off the gold at the corners.

Boxed couching is circular couching that starts on the outside and fills to the inside, with each row bricked to the next. As you approach the center, the couching stitches will get closer together to make the tighter turns.

1. Use one strand of red-orange couching thread to couch one pair of size 4 or 5 Japanese gold along the outer edge of the leaf. Couch clockwise and turn sharp corners (see page 38 for instructions).

2. When the outer edge is complete, don't sink the threads. Instead, continue to couch inside the first row. The first and second rows should be a couching needle width apart. A minute amount of the ground fabric shows between the rows of couching so that the rows don't overlap each other when the fabric is removed from the frame. When the work is unframed, the rows will appear closer together.

3. Brick the second row to the first row.

4. When you approach the corner of the first row, the second row corner should line up perfectly with the first row corner, stitch for stitch. This creates a slightly open pattern.

5. Couch each row so the corners line up to form the open pattern. It's not unusual to do the last row with a half pair.

PAINTED CANVAS

LEE

A hand-painted canvas before and after stitching. Stitched with a combination of needlepoint stitches and a variety of threads, the finished piece is a jewelry case.
Design and case from Lee's Needle Arts, Inc.

A painted canvas is just what the name implies – an artist's painting done on needlepoint canvas. The detail the artist paints on the canvas provides the stitcher with a wonderful foundation and lots of opportunity for embellishment. The artist paints a specific color on the intersections of the canvas, eliminating the guesswork of which color goes where. Before painted canvases, this precision was only available by following a stitch-by-stitch chart where it was necessary to concentrate on the stitch placement, leaving little flexibility to change the stitch or the thread. A painted canvas gives the stitcher the luxury of concentrating on a variety of threads and stitches instead of on transferring individual stitches to the ground fabric.

Painted canvases can be used for pillows, ornaments, stand-up dolls, chair seats, rugs, framed artwork, Christmas stockings, birth announcements, wall hangings, and much more.

You may be most familiar with painted canvases that come as kits that include the threads and stitching instructions but you can also buy hand-painted canvases that allow you the freedom to choose your own threads and stitches to personalize the canvas to your taste. Kits are widely available. One-of-a-kind or limited edition hand-painted canvases can be purchased in independent needlepoint shops. There are a variety of stitch books on the market to assist you in choosing threads and stitches, or you can take a class at a needlework shop. Most shops that sell hand-painted canvases have someone on the staff to help you choose threads and assist with the stitch placement.

In the past, stitchers have had to compartmentalize stitching techniques into embroidery, needlepoint, white work, stump work, etc. On a painted canvas all these techniques can be used in the same project. Because the design is already on the canvas, you have the freedom to concentrate on embellishing the design. The artwork on the canvas usually defines the direction and type of stitch and the painted color delineates the change in motif.

In the 30 years I've owned a needlework store, I have seen many painted canvases and have a great deal of respect for the painters and designers. These talented artists create a multitude of wonderful designs, which become more sophisticated and detailed each year. They have elevated the painted canvas to the level of art. Their attention to detail and the exquisite designs and shapes provide stitchers with a great road map for stitching. Some canvases are so well painted they could stand on their own, without ever having a thread placed on them.

CHAPTER 6:
TOOLS AND MATERIALS FOR PAINTED CANVAS

A stitched and unstitched painted canvas. The finished piece is embellished with bugle beads, silk theads, metallics, and decorative stitches.

Design by A Collection of Designs. Stitched by Nancy Cox.

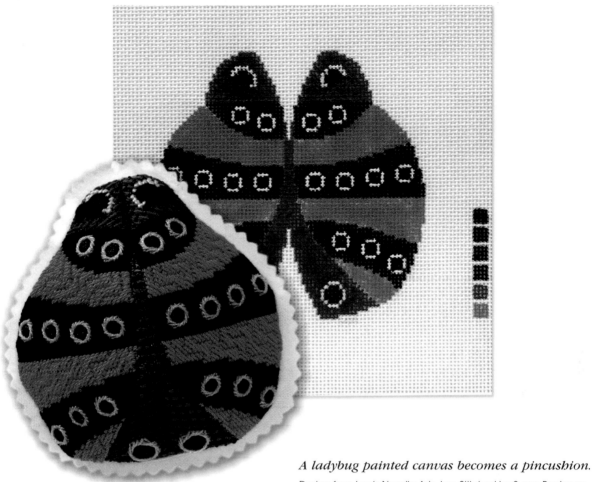

A ladybug painted canvas becomes a pincushion.
Design from Lee's Needle Arts, Inc. Stitched by Susan Beckman.

Ground Fabrics

Until the 1960s, most canvas work was done on *duo canvas* or *double mesh canvas*, which had two threads woven vertically and horizontally. The dual warp threads running parallel to the selvage were woven closer together than the dual weft threads. If the stitcher worked over the dual canvas threads, it was called *gross point*. If the stitcher elected to separate the dual threads and cover each thread individually, it was *petite point*. If the duo canvas counted 10 dual threads per inch, it would count 20 threads per inch when separated, which offered the advantage of stitching the background in a large stitch and stitching other areas in greater detail.

The wool thread available at the time was traditionally tapestry wool, which worked well in the duo canvas 10 threads per inch. It did not split or separate easily so its use was limited to certain canvas counts.

Today, duo canvas is most frequently seen with the design area already stitched, with only the background left for the stitcher to fill in. You may also run across canvases that have been silk-screened. In this process, the colors do not transfer precisely to the grid of the canvas, leaving you to decide which color goes on which intersection.

In the 1960s and '70s white mono canvas became

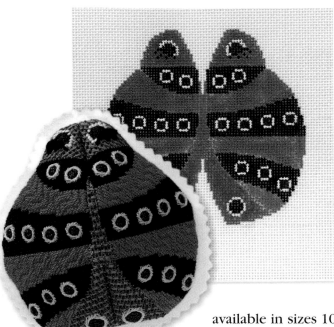

available in sizes 10, 12, 14, 18, and 24 threads per inch. Also newly available at that time was Persian wool, a two-ply wool in three-strand lengths that could be separated and used as one, two, or three strands in the needle. Persian wool is still widely used for stitching needlepoint projects. Many stores sell it by the strand, making it ideal for small pockets of color. The general rule is to use three strands for 10-count canvas, two or three strands for 12- or 14-count, and one strand for 18-count.

Hint

To find "threads per inch," lay a measuring tape or ruler parallel with a row of holes on the canvas. Place the inch marker on a hole and count the number of canvas threads between inch markers. Most mono canvases are 10 to 24 threads per inch.

When making an upright vertical stitch, the wool should be thicker (more strands) than a stitch on the diagonal. Because Persian wool is three-stranded, the number of strands can be changed to accommodate the different stitches. Different color strands of Persian wool can also be combined in the needle for shading.

As the popularity of canvas work grew, more artists painted canvases and more threads became available to embellish the canvases. Today the sophistication of the painting and the hundreds of threads available add to the excitement of embellishing a painted canvas.

Painted canvases are primarily painted on mono canvas, size 10 to 24 threads per inch. Mono canvas comes in a variety of colors so the designs are not necessarily painted on white canvas. One of the great advantages of colored canvas is that you can leave the canvas exposed, so it's not necessary to stitch the background.

A painted canvas framed up on a roller frame.

Frames

For decorative threads and stitches it is best to frame up your canvas on a roller frame or artist stretcher bars rather than try to hold the canvas in your hands. Hoops are not recommended for canvas work. See page 22 for instructions on how to use a roller frame.

Artist stretcher bars are usually purchased in pairs at needlepoint or art stores. Their primary function is to stretch artist's canvas for painting.

Measure the length and width of your canvas edge (the canvas size, not the design size). If your canvas measures 10" x 12", buy one 10" pair of stretcher bars and another 12" pair. The assembly is tongue and groove so they go together very easily.

Place the canvas on top of the stretcher bars and use a staple gun or long thumbtacks to secure it to the bars. After the canvas is secured, cover the raw edge with artist's tape or strapping tape (not masking tape). As the project progresses the staples/thumbtacks can loosen and the canvas can become spongy on the bars. If this happens, remove the staples or tacks and restretch and tighten the canvas.

A selection of the wide variety of threads that can be used to embellish a painted canvas.

Threads

Silk Threads

Silks have a natural beauty of their own. They are usually stranded with six to 12 strands per thread and are available in a large variety of colors, divided into color families.

A family of colors runs from the darkest value (the change from darkness to lightness) of a hue to the lightest value. Silk color families can have as few as four values or as many as eight values of the color.

Silk has a very smooth surface, which can be laid very flat on the canvas. When it's laid in opposing directions, it gives off wonderful reflections of light. It is the strongest of natural fibers and wears very well on canvas work.

Overdyed threads.

Twisted Silks

Twisted silks come in a variety of colors that give a more textural effect than the stranded silks. Twisted silks are available in different sizes to fit a specific canvas count. The advantage of using twisted silks is that you can work with them without having to strand them and lay them with a laying tool.

Cotton Threads

Six-stranded cotton floss is the most common cotton thread and is the most readily available in a great range of colors and color families. It works very well on painted canvas. Its greatest advantage is that it comes in more than 400 colors. Its affordability is also a factor, since some painted canvases require 30 or 40 colors.

Perle Cotton

Perle cotton is softly twisted 100% cotton that is available in a wide selection of colors. Size 12 is the smallest and size 3 is the largest. Sizes 12 and 8 are put up in balls and are not as suitable for canvas as sizes 5 and 3, which usually come in skeins (size 5 can sometimes be found in balls). Generally size 3 perle cotton fits 14-count canvas and size 5 fits 18-count canvas.

The color numbers correspond to those of six-stranded cotton floss, which is helpful when you want to change textures but not colors, although perle isn't available in as many colors as six-stranded cotton.

Overdyed and Variegated Threads

Overdyed threads are dyed with darker or lighter values of the original color or with a different color entirely. Purchase overdyed threads in sufficient quantity to finish your project because they are very susceptible to dye lot changes.

Variegated threads begin as white cotton or silk threads and the hue of the color is repeated in a sequence of light value to dark value. The color change is repeated in a set pattern so you can accurately predict how the finished stitching will look. Variegated threads can be found in both six-stranded and perle cottons.

With overdyed threads, the color change is less predictable and much more subtle, which is wonderful for shading. Overdyed threads are a good choice for leaves, sky, sand, and grass.

Linen Threads

Linen threads come in a variety of colors and are very workable on canvas. They give a wonderful textural look. I like to use them for tree trunks, wood surfaces, sandy beach areas, and anywhere the motif should exhibit some roughness.

Hint

I usually recommend that you stitch the design area first, then choose the thread for the background. The design area comes alive with the addition of thread and may no longer be compatible with the background color you selected before you started stitching. Some stitchers believe that if you leave the background for last, you won't finish it, but today it is perfectly acceptable to not stitch it at all, stitch only a portion of it, or fill it with a quick stitch.

Novelty Threads

Novelty threads include fuzzy threads, ribbon threads, silk and wool combinations, rayon, rayon with woven-in metallic, velvets, and many more. The selection grows with each passing year and each new thread brings excitement and new ideas.

One of the great joys of doing a painted canvas is selecting the threads. Most independent needlepoint stores are happy to assist in this process. Always buy enough – novelty threads come in dye lots, which are sometimes hard to match. This is especially true of hand-dyed or overdyed threads. It is very important to buy enough thread to complete the background for the same reason.

Metallic Threads

If a thread is referred to as *metallic* and *stitchable,* it means that the content of the thread is synthetic, not real metal. If the thread is referred to as a *metal* thread, it has some real metal content such as gold or silver or a mixture of metals. These are most likely to be nonstitchable threads and will tarnish with age.

Metallic threads are made with synthetic materials that glisten like metal and add pizzazz to the piece (shine to a lake, glint to snow, sparkle to a Christmas tree). Metallics won't tarnish or age and come in a wide range of colors and varieties that include braids, ribbons, and twists in different sizes.

Needles

The best needles for canvas work are blunt-end tapestry needles. Use a size 18 needle for 10-count canvas, size 20 for 12-count canvas, size 22 needle for 14-count canvas, and size 24 for 18-count canvas and congress (24 threads to the inch).

If you are stitching with a novelty thread that works better with a sharp needle, use a chenille needle that follows the same size needle chart.

A needle threader can be very helpful, especially for novelty threads.

Accessories

Scissors

Two pairs of sharp pointed embroidery scissors are a must for the canvas worker. You will use one to cut all of your threads except metallics. Use the second pair only for metallics because they will become too dull to cut other threads.

Stitch Book

There are many excellent books that teach a variety of stitches. How do you know which book is right for you? Visit your local bookstore or independent needlework shop and look at several books. Most stitch books are composed of charts of stitches. Examine the charts to see which are the easiest to follow. Then look at the content of the book. Does it have pictures of the finished stitches? This may or may not be important to you.

Some books have stitch charts with suggestions for where to place the stitches. This is helpful if you are a novice because it gives you an idea of what stitches work best in certain areas.

Pay special attention to how the stitches are illustrated. Are they numbered? (Most are not.) Are they comfortable for you to read and use? Does the book teach only needlepoint stitches or are there combinations of techniques?

If you are you planning to carry the book in your stitching bag, select a small one that is easily portable.

Choose the book that fits your needs, but realize that most needleworkers usually end up with more than one book. There are dozens on the market and once you get started, one book just won't be enough.

Magnifying Lens and Lights

There are a variety of lenses and lights on the market. If you stitch where there is a good source of light, you may not need either of these.

Laying Tool

A laying tool, as shown on page 19, is a must for laying multi-stranded threads on painted canvas. See page 81 for instructions on how to use one.

Markers

Use pigma markers if you need to mark the canvas. This is critical because pigma inks penetrate the starch on the canvas surface, which is important in case you need to block and stretch the piece back to its original shape after it's completed. To accomplish blocking and stretching, you will apply stream or moisture to the canvas. If the marker ink hasn't penetrated the starch, the moisture will cause the ink to float and it will wick into your stitches, which will leave a permanent spot on the work.

Test all markers before using them on canvas. Make a mark close to the canvas selvage, stitch white thread on top of the mark, then dampen it and see if the marker ink comes through the thread. If it does, change to a pigma marker.

CHAPTER 7:
TECHNIQUES FOR STITCHING ON PAINTED CANVAS

Stripping Stranded Threads

Silk threads and cotton floss make better stitches if the strands are separated, then placed back together before stitching. The threads lay flatter and give off more sheen. When you examine a piece of thread, you will see that the strands are twisted together, which does not make for a precise stitch. Separated strands lie flatter, give better light play, and provide better and wider coverage of the canvas.

The size of the canvas, the type of stitch, and the thickness of the paint on the canvas all affect the number of strands needed to complete the stitch.

1. Hold a single thread in your left fingers, letting the thread hang down vertically.

2. Use the fingers of your right hand to gently pull up one strand until it is free of the remaining strands.

3. Lay the single strand on a flat surface.

Note: *If the original thread has pulled or curled up, straighten it before you pull the next strand free.*

4. Pull out the next strand and lay it alongside the first strand.

5. Continue to pull the strands until you have the number you will use. Store the remaining strands for later use.

6. Combine the strands in the needle for stitching.

Using the Laying Tool

After you've stripped the strands, you will use a laying tool to straighten the strands as you stitch. When I first started to stitch with multiple strands, it became apparent that the strands needed to lie side-by-side for maximum beauty and light play. Using an ordinary embroidery needle, I had difficulty keeping the threads aligned and my hand cramped. I experimented with a rug needle, and even a small letter opener to eliminate the cramping, but with little success. Then I made my first trip to Japan and observed Japanese embroiderers at work. When I saw them using laying tools, I knew that my trip had been worthwhile.

The Japanese word for this tool is tekobari (stroking needle). Since that trip, I have used a BLT, the American version of tekobari, which is slightly bigger and squared off on the nonstroking end so that it doesn't roll on the ground fabric (when you put it down, it stays in place).

Laying tools are available at needlework shops for under $20 and work well with multi-stranded spun threads and filament threads such as flat silk.

1. Bring the threaded needle straight up the full length of the thread, keeping the needle's eye facing you. Practice to train your finger to feel and correctly position the needle's eye when the needle is at the back of the ground fabric. Pull the thread taut.

2. If the thread is twisted, spin the needle between your thumb and forefinger to straighten it. Tug the thread sharply to tighten the thread on the back of your work. This tug sets the stitch on the back and allows you to relax the thread on the top.

Hint

It is just as important to tighten the thread on the back of your work as it is on the front.

3. Take the needle down through the ground fabric until there is a 2" loop of thread on the surface of the ground fabric.

Hint

Some silks and novelty threads will snag and fuzz if you drag them across the canvas. Hold the thread above and away from the canvas rather than dragging it against the canvas.

4. Insert the laying tool into the loop and gently stroke the thread *in the direction of the stitch* to separate the strands. If you stroke back and forth, you will fuzz the thread. It should only take two or three strokes to straighten the strands. The strands should reenter the canvas side-by-side, not overlapping. (Fig. 1)

Hint

If the strands don't straighten in two or three strokes, it may be that the thread was twisted when going down or was brought up twisted. When you stroke the thread, all the strands should lie side-by-side and reenter the canvas with equal tension.

5. Complete the stitch, pulling the needle tight on the underside of the ground fabric to maintain tension. Place the laying tool on the base of the stitch to hold the stitch in place.

6. Bring the needle to the surface, halfway up in the opening in the ground fabric. The needle will stay in place. With your bottom hand, tightly hold the thread on the underside of the

Starting a Thread

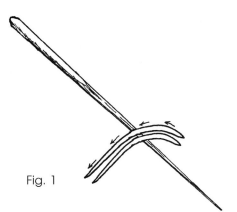

Fig. 1

ground fabric so it creates tension on the top stitch. Remove the laying tool.

7. Still holding the bottom thread, pick up the needle with your top hand. Pull the thread to the surface (it will be apparent if there is a knot in the bottom thread). When the thread is completely at the top, use your bottom hand to make sure the thread is flat on the underside.

8. When the thread is fully on the top, give it an extra tug to ensure proper tension on the top and bottom of the stitch.

Hint

Pulling the thread on top of the work is called "setting the stitch" and is the one of the most strategic parts of laying a thread flat, especially flat silk.

9. Repeat the process with all multi-strand stitches.

1. If your thread is multi-stranded, separate it to the desired number of strands before threading the needle with the number of strands you desire.

2. Make a small knot in the end of the thread and trim below the knot.

3. Place the knot on top of the canvas 1" from where you will begin stitching but in the path of your stitching.

Hint

Never place the knot too far from the starting point, planning to later cut off the knot and weave the end of the thread back through your work. This disturbs your work on the front of the canvas. Always place the knot in the path to be stitched. Placing the knot in another area may pick up unwanted colored threads.

4. After placing the knot on the right side of your work, make a pinhead stitch before starting the first stitch. Place the pinhead stitch in an area that will later be covered by stitching, never in an unstitched area. The pinhead stitch creates proper tension on the starting thread.

a. To make a pinhead stitch, bring the needle to the front of the work where it will be covered by your stitching.

b. Bring the needle up, then back down in a hole next door, *either vertically or horizontally, never over* an intersection. If you are using uncounted ground fabric, bring the needle to the top, then go back down extremely close to the up stitch.

c. The resulting stitch should be the size of a pinhead (very small), covering one thread of the canvas or a very small area of uncounted ground fabric. This small stitch should disappear into the ground fabric. It can easily be stitched over when stitching in this area. This stitch locks the beginning thread in place and assures it will stay embedded in the body of the work.

Hint

If your first stitch is an upright gobelin on canvas, make the pinhead stitch one thread under the start of your first stitch. This will make your first stitch straight. If you started from the waste knot without a pinhead stitch, the first upright stitch would slant toward the knot. If your first stitch is a satin stitch, place the pinhead under the first satin stitch.

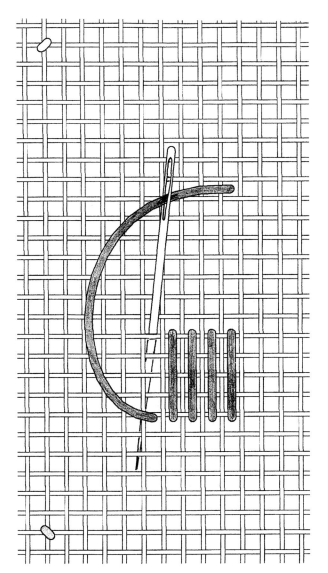

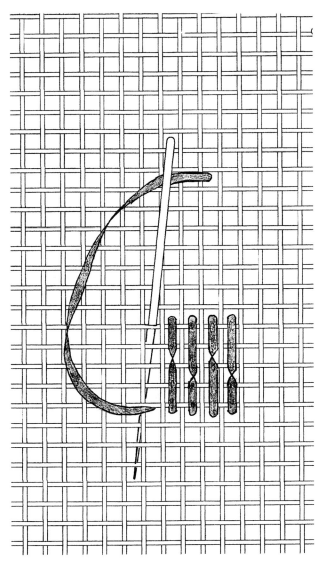

Fig. 2. The correct needle position. Notice that the angle of the needle allows you to see through the eye.

Fig. 3. If you can't see through the eye, the thread will twist.

Holding the Needle

When stitching, carefully feel the needle underneath the work. Place your thumb and forefinger to hold the eye side so that as the needle comes to the surface, the eye will come up so you can see through it. This will bring the thread to the surface parallel with the stitch, straight up and untwisted. Complete the stitch and take the needle back down, still keeping the eye facing you. This will maintain straight threads.

Ending a Thread

End the thread with two pinhead stitches. These can be stitched in an adjacent area that will be stitched later or can be done by bringing the needle up through your finished stitching. Most people are worried that two pinhead stitches will not actually hold the work. Test it by stitching two pinhead stitches and trying to pick them out. It's not easy. This is how Oriental embroiderers end their threads.

Hint

If you put the two pinhead stitches in finished stitching, they will each create a gap in the stitched area. Take the needle back down in the open gap, covering one canvas thread or making a small stitch in uncounted ground fabric. Pull tight on the needle and the gap will close, making the pinhead stitch invisible.

1. Make one pinhead stitch and pull the thread tight on the back of the work so the stitch becomes invisible. Make a second pinhead stitch close to the first one.

Hint

This is a firm rule: Start with one pinhead stitch and end with two. Always make two ending pinhead stitches. This is how all Japanese embroidery is started and stopped (with the exception of starting a couching thread where the knot is very small and placed on the back of the work).

2. Bring the thread to the front of your work close to the last pinhead stitch and cut off the thread.

This method works beautifully if you want to make six or 10 stitches in an area, then start a new color. You can start and stop in the same color area. Think of several white stars in a dark blue field. This method allows you to stop and start in the white areas and not carry the white through the blue background.

Hint

Stopping with two pinhead stitches won't work in a piece stitched in basketweave or if the thread is a heavy braid (such as #16). However, it works beautifully when stitching cross-stitch with 30 or 40 colors. Weaving back through the back of such a work would produce a thick matted back.

Choosing the Right Canvas

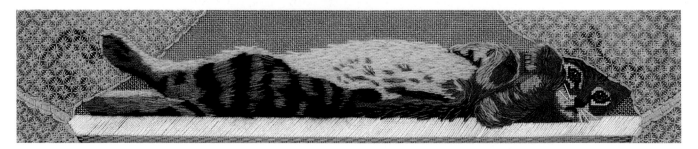

With so many wonderful painted canvases on the market, how do you choose one that is right for you?

If you are a beginner, choose a painted canvas with few details, with blocks of colors, and minimal shading. This will make it easier to fill the colored areas with stitches. When you are starting out you might like to do a small piece and graduate to a bigger canvas for a pillow or Christmas stocking. There are many small canvases available for ornaments, box tops, eyeglass cases, purses, and belts.

For children, choose simple geometric blocks of color they can fill with long straight satin stitches done from one painted edge to the next. This technique is sometimes available in kits and is called *long stitch*. Long stitching is fun and can be the beginning of a lifetime of enjoyable stitching.

Even though I recommend simple designs for beginners, I have learned not to be too restrictive. A cross-stitcher who had never stitched on a painted canvas came into my store and fell in love with a very beautifully shaded cat canvas with a large geometric border. It was a big piece, about 16" x 16", and she was ready to go home with it but I felt it was too ambitious for a beginner and discouraged her from buying it. She loved cats (and this was one great cat) and she insisted on buying the canvas, so I suggested she bring it to a class before she started to stitch. In class, we chose a thin fuzzy thread in colors to match the cat and she started stitching the darkest value. I showed her how to do random long and short stitches on the dark shadings. The stitches followed how the artist had painted the cat on the canvas. When she had completed the darkest value, I had her follow the paint of the lightest value in the cat, just covering the canvas with random satin stitches. When she had completed these two values, she filled the open areas on the cat with random split stitches in the medium value.

After finishing the stitching, she used a small brush to gently brush the furry stitches to raise the nap and fuzz up the stitches more.

The cat turned out great, partly because it was painted so realistically and partly

Random long and short stitches were used on the cat's body. The dark colors were stitched first, then the lightest colors, then filled with medium colors.
Design by Tapestry Tent, stitched by Eleanor Gibson.

because the fuzzy thread was very forgiving and blended the stitches together.

This taught me that if you truly love the canvas, you should buy it. Throw caution to the wind, select a canvas you like, and adjust the threads and stitches to your skill level. After all, you are doing it for your own enjoyment and I have yet to encounter the needlepoint police.

The gauge of the canvas is an important decision. Can you comfortably work on canvas that's 18 threads to the inch or would you feel better working with a bigger canvas such as 12 or 14 threads to the inch?

If you are choosing a canvas for a specific purpose such as the top of a stool, examine the design. Will it look good from all directions? Will it fit well on the stool? Will there be enough excess canvas to go around the stool?

The eyes were stitched with metallic threads in a tent stitch. To create a realistic look, the lace curtain was stitched with the diamond eyelet stitch over the painted ears. The paint on the canvas peeks through the stitch to make the ears appear to be behind the curtain.

Color is also an important consideration. Will the thread colors fit in the décor of your home? Don't despair if you love the design but can't use the colors specified. You can change the color of the canvas by following the instructions that follow.

Right Canvas, Wrong Colors

It's easy to change the colors of a painted canvas if you use the *value scale*. For example, on the value scale the red hue is divided into values of light to dark. The lightest value of red is usually referred to as #1 (palest pink), which gets progressively darker as the number rises to #9 (reddish black). This progression occurs when different amounts of white and black are added to the red hue. So, if a flower on the canvas is painted in four values of red, you can easily change the red to four values of purple if you change each individual value equally. It is helpful to work with the actual skeins of thread when comparing the values and replacing one color with another. Your design will stay balanced, just the way the artist intended, but you will have the color you want.

Hint

If an area is painted with a dark value of a hue, it is not possible to cover the paint with a light value of the same hue or a different light hue. The dark paint will shadow through the lighter color on top.

Mixing Colors Optically

You can create an "optical color blend" by stitching with fewer strands than you need to completely cover the paint and letting the color of the canvas show through. When you view the area, your eye mixes the two colors – the thread and the canvas – and blends them.

Another way to accomplish this blending is to stitch the thread thick enough to cover the paint but stitch every other row of the stitch pattern or leave out a step of the stitch. In the case of the cat, the curtain was covered with diamond stitches in a light hue so the paint of the ears and tail would shadow through the curtain.

The ears and tail were never stitched and the painted canvas peeks through.

Stitching on Painted Canvas

After you've chosen the painted canvas, the next step is to select threads. You don't need to select all the threads at once – start with just a few. You also need to decide what stitch to use in each area. Does the thread work well for the stitch? Select one or two stitches and experiment. I usually start on a section of the canvas that seems interesting and try a few thread choices with a single stitch. If the stitch doesn't look right, try a different one until you find the one you like.

Finding the Starting Point

Choose an area in the foreground of the design as the starting point. As you stitch you will automatically make that area slightly bigger, which is exactly how it should be because the foreground should be bigger than the background.

Hint

While you are stitching the canvas, the stitches are very close to your eyes. To get a better sense of how the stitch and color look, place the piece across the room and view it from a distance. This little test will help you immensely in determining if the threads and stitches work together.

This charming painted canvas was stitched with needlepoint stitches and embellished with a lace appliqué skirt, stump work wings, and ribbon bows.
Design from A Collection of Designs. Stitched by Nancy Cox.

Some canvases may have more than one possibility for a starting place. For example, in a large Christmas stocking, there are several equally important features, so choose the one that is most important to you.

Alternatively, you may want to start in an area where you feel comfortable with the stitch you've designated for that area.

Choosing the Stitch

Get your stitch book out – there are hundreds of stitches to choose from. Think about the elements of the design. In small areas, choose a small compact stitch that fits in the area. If the area is large, you have more room to do a bigger textured stitch.

Keep a notebook of ideas. Stitch a variety of stitches on a piece of blank canvas to see how the stitches look. Stitch the same stitch with different threads. This will give you a feel for working with the threads and will illustrate how different a stitch can look done in different threads. Jot down what you think or where you have used the stitch or thread previously. Create your own stitch book.

There will be times when you experiment with a stitch and it doesn't work out. Be prepared to take it out and call it a learning experience. Remember, there are no mistakes – only learning experiences.

Design from Tapestry Tent Design.

If a stitch does not come to mind for a specific area, start stitching in a different, simpler area and think about the problem area while you are stitching. Often an idea will take shape and off you will go.

Tips for Choosing Stitches

• Trees, shrubs, small flowers, rocks, and walls should be done in stitches that have some height to them. These are usually stitches that have one or more layers of threads. A simple cross stitch falls into this category. Trees and bushes are not smooth, so select a textured stitch.

• Flowers are wonderful done in French knots, lazy daisy stitches, bullion stitches, or worked with ribbon threads.

• Water, beaches, and grassy areas work well in stitches that are stitched horizontally so they seem to flow in the direction the water flows. It's especially effective to accentuate the horizontal stitches with overdyed threads because water and sand would not necessarily be all the same color.

• Skies can be worked in overdyed thread with darning titches because sky is neutral to the design (unless it's

stormy). For skies, choose a stitch that falls into the background of the piece rather than one with a lot of texture. Skies can be stitched either vertically or horizontally but should be flat. Silk threads work wonderfully for skies because you can use one less strand than normal and let the thread recede into sky.

• Shaded flowers are generally stitched in tent stitches that follow the shading. However, I use the tent stitch as a last resort for shaded flowers. Shaded flowers can be stitched in long and short stitches, brick stitches, outline stitches, split stitches, or interlocking gobelins – all stitches that produce a shaded effect.

• Large color blocks are perfect for geometric stitches. If they turn in opposing directions, choose a six-stranded floss or silk to give maximum light play.

Choosing stitches is part of the fun of working a painted canvas. Choosing a stitch or a thread may be trial-and-error but with every try, you will learn something.

Remember, you can't make a mistake because it is *your* canvas and what *you* think goes. I consider a painted canvas much like a recipe and just as I might add more cinnamon or decrease the amount of sugar, I make adjustments to the painted canvas. It can be stitched all in continental stitch, partly in continental, or fully stitched with decorative stitches and threads. That is the beauty of a painted canvas.

Compensating

One of the difficulties beginners encounter is that needlepoint stitches don't conform exactly to the colored area on the canvas and so must be adjusted to fit. Don't panic! Simply shorten the stitch to fit within the painted area.

Outlining an Area

Often an area on the painted canvas will show a black outline. If the black line is faint, it is probably the original tracing of the artist and is not meant to be stitched as an outline. However, if the black line is a single black painted thread of canvas, it is meant to be stitched as an outline and should not be included in the colored area.

When stitching a single black outline, it seems logical to cover the line with a continental stitch, but experience has shown that the continental stitch leaves gaps as it rounds some of the curves. This isn't a big problem – at a distance these openings or gaps are filled in by your eye and won't detract from the overall work. However, the black line can be successfully covered with an embroidery stitch such as an outline, chain stitch, or backstitch, or can be couched with a metallic braid. These stitches produce smoother lines that are more pleasing to the eye and eliminate any open areas.

CHAPTER 8:
PAINTED CANVAS EXAMPLES

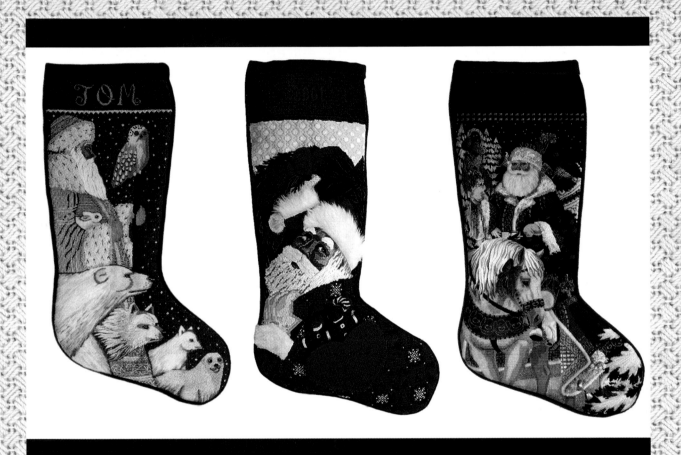

Example #1: Arctic Santa Stocking

The first sample painted canvas is a Christmas stocking with a lot of detail. With all painted canvases, you stitch the foreground area first. By stitching what is up front in the design first, you make it bigger and bring it forward. In this design, the polar bear is in front of Santa and the other animals, making it a good place to start stitching.

Being in the foreground, the bear needs to come forward, so you want to use a thread and stitch that will accomplish that. The obvious thread choice for the bear is a fuzzy thread, but the stitch selection is harder. You need a stitch that will mimic the way the hair on the bear would realistically lay. A square stitch or a stitch with a lumpy texture just wouldn't look right. Neither would a repeat geometric stitch. You need a stitch that will create the appearance of hair. The answer: random

"Arctic Santa," designed by Liz Goodrick Dillon, Tapestry Tent Designs. Stitched by Sue Kilkenney.

long and short stitches that will flow and move with the contours of the body.

Stitch the nose and eyes with a continental stitch. It's nice to stitch the eyes in a metallic to add a bit of sparkle. I often satin stitch the nose with a patent leather thread to add some shine.

Hint

When "painting with a needle" (which is what you are doing), make your stitches fairly long. Shorten them on curves and lengthen them on straight-aways. Stitches that are too short appear choppy and don't flow well for shading.

Note that the stitched bear has a dark value along the edges. This dark thread lifts the bear off the other motifs in the stocking. This is the same as a black outline except it is thicker in some areas. It has the same effect as an outline, which distinguishes one motif from another. Leaving an open space or void, as you would do on a fabric ground, is not successful on canvas – it looks like you missed some of the canvas. Even if the artist didn't paint an area with an outline effect, you can always add it. You will encounter many painted canvases where one motif blurs into another. When this happens, stitch both motifs fully, then use one strand of black cotton floss to stitch a running stitch at the junction of the two motifs. The gap between the running stitches won't be obvious, and more importantly, the running stitches will separate the motifs.

Stitch the other animals in this stocking with textured threads and stitches that simulate hair, such as split stitches, interlocking gobelins, rows of outline stitches, and random satin stitches. It's not necessary to stick with one thread type. In fact, it's very effective to combine a thin fuzzy thread with one strand of fine crewel wool. This combination of threads also lets you blend two subtle shades of white or gray with whatever color the animal is painted.

There is a very simple way to lift one motif off another in a painted canvas or embroidered piece. Use one or two strands of dark floss and work a single row of outline stitches along the edge of the motif that you wish to bring forward.

The rabbit in this design could easily be overshadowed by the stitching in Santa's coat. Because the rabbit is outlined with one strand of dark blue wool, it appears to be tucked into Santa's arm and its shape and ears are still defined.

The outline around the rabbit brings it forward and lifts it off the rest of the design.

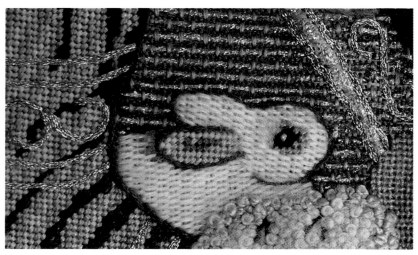

The foreground wolf is brought forward by the use of a dark thread outline to separate it from surrounding motifs. The ears are stitched in tent stitches then outline stitches in the same color as the tent stitches.

The stitches and threads chosen for the seal bring him forward from the surrounding area and make it look like he's in front of the background wolf.

Note the dark wool thread along the back of the foreground wolf's body and how it makes the wolf jump out at you. If this area were stitched in a light color, the wolf and everything else would run together and lose definition.

In this example, sections of the wolf's face are stitched in tent stitches because the hair in this area would naturally be shorter and precise. The stitches are lengthened gradually from the face outward, following the contour of the body. Stitch the dark color first to serve as a guideline for the filling stitches. Then stitch the lightest colors and finally, fill the remaining areas with the medium value colors.

Stitch the seal with split stitches in silk or floss and add an outline stitch in a dark color to bring it forward. Seal fur isn't fuzzy, so this creates a smoother effect.

Hint

There are times when it is not necessary to outline all the way around the motif. It is sometimes sufficient to make the dark outline only where needed to separate two motifs.

Faces are usually stitched with tent stitches. When many color values are used, experienced stitchers combine both continental and the basketweave stitches in the face. Half cross-stitches are seldom used in the face area because they don't look as crisp as continental and basketweave stitches. There are other stitches that will work (interlocking gobelins, split stitches, satin stitches), but if the face has very detailed shading, the stitch should be basic and easy to do.

Because of the many subtle color changes, DMC six-stranded cotton (floss) is a good choice for any shaded area. DMC comes in 400 colors so it is easy to find threads for all the subtle color changes. If necessary, more than one color thread can be used in the needle for even more delicate shading. When shading a face in continental stitches, don't use values that are too far apart or the result will be blotchy-looking.

When selecting floss colors for shading, take the painted canvas to a needlework store and test the color of each floss skein against the paint on the canvas. Once you have made your selections, ask permission to look at the skeins in daylight and see if they truly match the paint. Store lights often distort colors and natural light is much better for choosing values of hues that are close together.

Stitch the darkest values on the face (the shadow areas) first. Then stitch the lightest value areas (the highlights). The

Santa's face is stitched with tent stitches and the beard with a combination of random long and short and outline stitches and textured thread.

remaining areas are closer in value and are the bridge between the light and dark. When changing from one color to another in these areas, mix the two colors in the needle to form a bridge between the two colors. For example, if you are using four strands of six-stranded cotton in the needle, when you transition from one color to another make the bridge stitches (stitches between the two colors) with two strands of each color. You only need a few bridge stitches between the two colors – just enough to "muddy" the area so the eye can't see where one color left off and the next one started. Don't make the bridge stitches in a straight line, but rather fill a random small area. Mixing strands allows you to have a great variety of values for shading.

Stitch the eyes with conti-

nental stitches. Using metallic braid in the eyes, especially the white spot and black pupil, will add life to the eyes.

Fuzzy silk, angora, Wisper, Medici, or overdyed wool are all good thread choices for beards and hair. The thread choice has a great effect on these areas. For a very fluffy beard, you can brush angora thread. Most Santas have a mustache with "growth" lines going in the opposite direction of the beard. Stitch mustache stitches, whether they are outline or split stitches, in the direction of the growth of the hair. The values of color are usually closer together in a mustache than in a beard because they have less textural changes.

There are numerous ways to stitch beards. First examine how the artist painted the beard. Use the dark growth lines as guidelines to shade the beard. These growth lines establish the contour of the beard. Stitch the growth lines with a stitch that will flow, such as an

outline stitch, split stitch, chain stitch, or satin stitch.

Start stitching the beard at the area closest to the face. With hair, start at the top of the head and stitch to the ends of the hair. Stitch in the direction the hair and beard would grow. Stitch the growth lines first. If the lines are wider than a single row of stitches, return to the top and make an adjacent line where it needs to be wider. Fill in between the growth lines with split stitches or other stitches, but always make long stitches to avoid a choppy look and make it look more like hair. These long stitches should be of uneven length and should not form any pattern. Stitch with a sharp needle and ignore the holes for this process.

Stitch the eyebrows along the growth lines of the hair and with a much more textured thread than the face. The textured thread brings the eyebrows forward and lifts them off the face.

Example #2: Gingerbread Men Stocking

Painted canvases don't have to be confined to canvas stitches alone. They can be a melting pot for all kinds of techniques. This sweet stocking illustrates the combination of needlepoint and appliqué.

A unique feature of this stocking is the heart-shaped pocket that holds the gingerbread men. The pocket is stitched on a separate piece of canvas and appliquéd to the stocking canvas. Note that the pocket is stitched in a needlepoint stitch. It doesn't really matter which geometric stitch you choose because it is a big red area. It could be a large stitch or a stitch with a rather lengthy repeat pattern because the surface is unmarred by lines or shapes. There are lots of stitches that will work. A blanket stitch around the pocket hides the appliqué stitches and decorates the edge. This pocket could hold real toys and candy canes at Christmas time.

In this example, instead of using stitching to finish the brim on Santa's hat and the

This clever stocking allows for a lot of variety in stitching, combining embroidery and needlepoint techniques.
"Gingerbread Men Stocking," designed by Liz Goodrick Dillon, Tapestry Tent Designs. Stitched by Susan Beekman.

cuffs of his coat, they are covered with pieces of fur-like fabric tacked onto the canvas. The trick to placing fabric on canvas is to hide the tacking stitches by carefully making tiny stitches with a sharp needle and invisible thread. This furry fabric can be fluffed at the seam line to hide the stitches. If the fabric is smooth, with no texture, run tacky glue around the edges to prevent raveling, let the glue dry, then stitch close to edge with small tacking stitches. Then couch a thread over the tacking stitches to hide the stitches. This is a great technique for a lady's gown or a trim around a neckline.

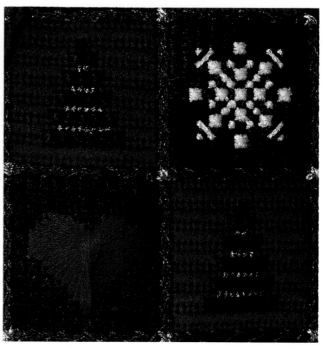

The gingerbread men were stitched separately, finished with fabric on the back, stuffed with cotton, and inserted into an appliqué pocket.

It's fun to fill small geometric areas with small compact repeat patterns.

These gingerbread men were worked on a separate canvas, then inserted into the heart-shaped pocket. Because the gingerbread men are small, they were worked in a very small geometric stitch with an easy repeat. The gingerbread men had to be bent to shape after they were stitched, so a long or large stitch wouldn't work because it would gap and show exposed canvas. A small, smooth, and compact stitch was used instead. The faces were adorned with button eyes and trim.

Each of the gingerbread men was stitched separately, finished, and inserted into the pocket.

The patchwork background behind the pocket is a very interesting area. The squares are treated as repeat patterns, with each Christmas tree, heart, and snowflake stitched the same way. Because the pocket, gingerbread men, and Santa are focal points on the stocking, the repeat patterns form a pleasant, unobtrusive background. These small areas lend themselves to small compact stitches and threads that will lay flat, such as silk, crewel wool, or six-stranded cotton. Because they are a background and need to recede, a full textured stitch and thread would not be appropriate. These squares appear more than once in this area so the stitches should be the same for each repeat square. It would be a mistake to treat each square as a sampler, which would make the whole area much too busy and detract from the main areas of the canvas.

Example #3: Santa on Horseback Stocking

A spectacular palette for stitching artistry, this stocking is sure to become a treasured heirloom. "Santa on Horseback," designed by Liz Goodrick Dillon, Tapestry Tent Designs. Stitched by Sue Kilkenney.

This truly beautiful stocking has special meaning to Sue Kilkenney, the stitcher, because she watched the artist, Liz Goodrick Dillon, paint the canvas from start to finish. Liz started with the horse, which is in the foreground, and thus should be the starting point for stitching. (It was interesting to note that artists conform to the "foreground first" rule too.)

Stitch the horse's mane first because it is on top of the body. It is important to stitch in the direction of the mane. The stitches in the mane should be bigger and more flowing than the hair on the horse's body. Horsehair is very smooth and shiny, where the mane is very flowing. Avoid using a too-fuzzy thread in the mane. It's better to delineate the flow with a silk thread that can be plied down to a fine strand to give the effect of the fine strands of a horse's mane. For the smooth horsehair, use a silky thread in a split stitch or an interlocking gobelin stitch.

Santa's face is stitched in tent stitches with DMC six-stranded cotton and Kreinik braid for the eye. The beard is stitched with Santa's Beard, Medici, and Wisper threads in a combination of split and random long and short stitches. His collar and hat brim are done with French knots.

This view gives you an idea of the variety of threads, textures, and stitches on one piece.

Examine Santa's hair and beard to find the dark growth lines the artist painted. The growth lines indicate the flow or the direction of the strands of hair. Stitch these lines first with linen, twisted silk, or a silk thread.

Stitch the random long and short stitches next. These outline stitches don't have to be stitched with the same thread as the rest of the beard. If stitched with something other than a fuzzy thread, they will be subtle and indicate how the beard should flow.

Once the outlines are stitched, fill in the areas between with a fuzzy thread or a combination of two threads such as a silk and Wisper, or a Medici wool and angora. Start at the face and stitch down-ward, completing all the stitches between two growth lines. Make your stitches random in length (it is very easy to slip into stitching all the same length). Keep your eyes on the flow of the beginning stitches to guide the flow of the hair or beard. Concentrate on only stitching between two guidelines. When that is finished, move to an adjacent growth line and fill between the next two. Keep stitching in this manner until the beard is finished.

Fine, silken hair such as would be found on an angel or a child could be stitched in this same manner. Instead of fuzzy thread, use a silk or six-stranded floss.

Stitch the white trim on Santa's coat with a very textured stitch and thread to lift it off the coat. Good stitch choices are brick stitches or French knots for a fuzzy texture. To give the jacket the look of velvet, use a velvet type thread. When stitching with a very textured thread such as velvet, choose a very simple stitch because the thread is so heavily textured that the contours of a complicated stitch are lost. Use a brick stitch or a Victorian step (one of my favorites).

Overdyed threads create a realistic look in the wreath.

Random long and short stitches make a regal cardinal nestled in the tree.

Stitch the wreath over Santa's arm with an overdyed green thread in an embroidery stitch to look like leaves. It could have been done just as successfully in bullion knots. This is a perfect place to use overdyed thread because a green wreath would not realistically be all one shade of green – it would have subtle color changes. In this area you wouldn't follow the color changes the artist painted, but would let the thread do the color changes.

This green wreath is embellished with red berries nestled into the greens. The berries could be beads rather than stitches.

A wonderful feature of this stocking is the red bird perched on the tree. Birds always lend themselves to an embroidery stitch instead of a squared needlepoint stitch. They are wonderful worked in soft crewel wool, stranded silk, or floss in random long and short stitches.

This face illustrates the subtle blending you can achieve with DMC floss in the tent stitch.

Design by Tapestry Tent. Stitched by Sue Kilkenney.

SHADING

The painted canvases in Section 2 were relatively easy to shade because the artist provided guidelines I call "growth lines." The growth lines show where to stitch the dark lines, the light areas, and where to fill in with medium values. For example, the dark shading in a beard becomes obvious if you first stitch the growth lines to see how the beard hairs flow. Stitching between the growth lines divides a large section into several smaller sections, which also makes the project more doable. Think of the adage "divide and conquer" and you'll understand. Growth lines divide the task into sensible, stitchable areas.

In Section 3, you will be shading on blank ground fabric, not canvas. Where the canvas showed you helpful growth lines, on ground fabric you will draw your own. It's easy and fun and will give you a great sense of accomplishment.

CHAPTER 9:
TOOLS AND MATERIALS FOR SHADING

*These morning glories were
stitched on Ro fabric, used as a
counted and uncounted ground.*

Ground Fabrics

Ground fabrics are divided into three categories:

1. Counted (needlepoint canvas, Aida cloth, Cashel linen, and many more).

2. Uncounted (linen twill, Belgium linen, or silk fabrics).

3. Fabrics that can be used as either counted or uncounted. Ro and Sha (see page 16) fall into this category because they are flexible enough to allow the stitcher to count some areas and treat some areas as an uncountable ground.

There is a lot of comfort in having predetermined holes to work with and not having to decide where to place the needle. On the other hand, the freedom to place your needle anywhere gives you the opportunity for much lovelier curved lines and edges of petals.

As you saw in the previous section, shading on painted canvas is done on a counted ground fabric such as needlepoint canvas, which offers established guidelines for the shading. In this section you will explore the art of shading on uncounted blank ground fabric. It is a much more daunting task to shade without the artist's guidelines, but once you are comfortable with some simple techniques, it's a lot of fun and will tap into your creativity.

Any closely woven material will work as uncounted ground fabric, but if you are planning to use silk threads, you should also use silk ground fabric. Test the thread by pulling it through the ground fabric and see if it wears the silk thread. If the thread pills or roughs up, use a larger needle.

Frame up the fabric to see if it stretches too much. If it distorts or stretches, it will not hold the threads properly. Some polyesters fall into this category.

Accessories

A sharp pair of scissors is an absolute must.

To frame up silk embroidery, you will need a Japanese frame or a roller frame. Framing up crewel embroidery or stitchery can be done on stretcher strips or in a hand-held hoop.

You'll need a laying tool for silk embroidery, but it's not necessary for crewel or stitchery.

Threads

The type of thread often defines the name of the embroidery. For example, *crewel embroidery* refers to the use of two-ply wool threads on linen twill or Belgium linen. If you are working with silk fabric and silk threads, that embroidery is called *silk embroidery.* If you are working with cotton and blended ground fabrics and six-stranded floss, knitting yarns, or perle cottons, you are doing *stitchery.*

The threads you use for shading on blank ground fabric are the same as you use for shading on canvas. Which ones you choose may vary depending on the motif. Use silk for flowers with subtle color changes. Use blends and overdyed threads for animals. Flat silk thread on silk ground fabric creates the ultimate shaded flowers.

Needles

When working on an uncounted ground, always use a sharp needle. There are many choices on the market.

Chenille needles are comparable to tapestry needles in size and shape, and are numbered the same way but have a much bigger eye and a sharp end. These are the needles of choice for crewel embroidery because you can easily thread the wool through the eye.

Embroidery needles or *sharp needles* are the type of needle you find in stitchery kits. They have a good size eye but are much longer than tapestry or chenille needles. They are sold in packages of size 1 to 5 (1 being the largest), or packages of size 3 to 9, or varying assortments.

Designs

There are many sources for designs. One of the most obvious is your own photographs. Take pictures of the flowers in your garden (or any garden), or look through a flower catalog. When you find a picture you like, blow it up to the design size you need to work with.

Another possible source is coloring books. Trace the design and transfer it to fabric. Magazines, picture books, and greeting cards are full of lovely photos and designs. Dover has a whole line of paperback books with line drawings. Check at the local bookstore for their books.

Train your eye to watch for interesting subjects.

CHAPTER 10:
TECHNIQUES FOR SHADING

Transferring the Design

To transfer designs to fabric, purchase transfer paper and follow the instructions on the package. Be very careful not to press your fingers or palms against the paper or your fingerprints will transfer along with the design. Saral transfer paper is a good choice because it comes in several colors, is wax free, and is reusable.

If your ground fabric is porous enough to see through, tape your design to the window and tape the fabric on top of the design. Trace the design on the fabric. I use a size 005 pigma pen to make a very thin line that won't rub off or smudge and is archival safe.

The pens also come in colors for colored fabrics. If you use a pencil, be sure it is a hard #4 pencil. Never use a soft pencil, as it will smudge. A white pencil can be used on black fabric.

My preferred method for transferring designs is by stitching rather than tracing. To use this method, frame up the piece on either a roller frame or a Japanese frame and copy the design onto tracing paper. Then place the tracing paper on the framed fabric using magnets to hold down the four corners of the design. Stitch over each line of the design with a running backstitch combination using silk couching thread close to the color of the ground fabric. Be sure to cover every line with these stitches. When you've stitched completely around the design, tear away the tracing paper. If the line is not pleasing, unpick the running stitch and move the line.

This pink flower was stitched with random long and short stitches with needlepoint silk and overdyed floss.

Pink Flower – Shading with Random Long and Short Stitches

Random long and short shading is easy to accomplish with a few guidelines.

Transfer the flower design to the fabric and examine the components of the flower – the center and the petals. The flower center is in the foreground and should be stitched first.

After stitching the center, determine which petal is foremost on the flower. That's the petal you should stitch first, after you've stitched the flower center.

Stitching the Yellow Center

1. The first step in stitching the yellow center is to lay a foundation. Use two strands of yellow needlepoint silk to lay long satin stitches parallel to the weft threads of the ground fabric. Lay the two strands close together, being careful not to encroach on the petal areas. Leave a little space between the center yellow stitches and the petals. A little blank fabric or void area makes the flower look more realistic.

2. Because the yellow foundation is made up of long satin stitches, you need to make sure

The temporary holding threads have been removed.

they stay in place. Do this with temporary holding threads. Thread one strand of yellow needlepoint silk in the needle and stitch a long stitch perpendicular to the foundation at 1/4" (5mm) intervals from one end of the foundation to the other.

3. Couch the temporary holding thread in place with the same thread, very softly and randomly. The temporary holding threads will be removed later but the couching stitches will remain.

4. As you can see in the photo, this flower center features gold metallic braid ribs on top of the foundation. Couch the braid in place with one strand of yellow silk (the same thread you used in the foundation). The couching method used here is referred to as *ara togi couching,* a precise method of couching I learned in Japan. It is the best method I have ever worked to couch a metallic thread to form a curve. It works wonderfully for veins on leaves and anywhere you need a couched curve. (Fig. 1)

5. Couch the dominant lines first. In this case the dominant lines are the two sides. Couch the metallic braid to form beautiful curves. Don't try to conform to the foundation stitches even if some peek out on the outside of the couched line. When the piece is displayed, the viewer will see the curved line, not the small stitches that are outside the line.

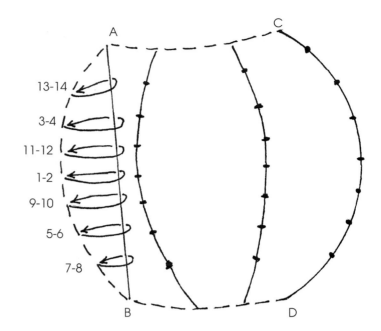

Fig. 1

6. Stitch the gold braid from the top of the foundation to the bottom of the foundation on one side (A to B). This forms a straight stitch.

7. Make a pinhead stitch and park the needle, ready to make the stitch on the other side, but don't make this stitch yet.

8. Thread a couching needle with one strand of yellow silk or one strand of gold couching thread. Knot the end of the thread and place the knot on the back of the stitched foundation. Come up through the foundation and make a pinhead stitch.

9. Bring the needle up at the center of the edge line, loop around the gold braid, and go down on the edge of the foundation (1 to 2).

10. In your mind's eye, divide the space between this center stitch (1 to 2) and (A). Make another loop stitch (3 to 4).

11. Divide the space from (1 to 2) and (B) and make a third loop stitch (5-6).

12. Continue until the line is couched with evenly spaced stitches.

13. Couch the other side.

14. Divide the remaining space into equal portions. The lines on the left curve to the left and the lines on the right curve to the right. If there's a center line, it can curve either way.

Marking Growth Lines on the Petals

1. Divide the foremost petal into stitching sections by marking growth lines. Growth lines make it easy to stitch from the outer edge to the center of the flower. To mark growth lines, find the center top of the petal and mark it with a straight pin. Find the center bottom of the petal and mark that point with another pin. Draw a line connecting these two points. On dark fabric, use a white pencil and on light fabric use a #4 pencil with a very light line. (Fig. 2)

> ### Hint
>
> Instead of marking, I prefer to stitch growth lines with running stitches of one strand of floss. I have found it difficult to adjust pencil or chalk lines, whereas the stitched line can be easily removed and restitched if adjustments are necessary. The stitch should reach from the top to the bottom of the petal and bisect the petal.

2. Divide the top of the petal from the center to the left edge. Do the same on the bottom of the petal. Connect these two center points with a line. You now have two stitching areas to the left of the center. Divide the area to the right of the center in the same manner. Divide all the areas in half again. You now have nine growth lines and 10 areas to stitch. Divide the two outermost areas in half (the dotted lines). The stitches in the areas outside the dotted lines may not reach the center of the petal.

3. Mark growth lines on each of the petals. I mark growth lines as I stitch each petal. If you start with every petal marked, the lines may get confusing. I usually stitch a petal, then mark the next petal to stitch and so on.

> ### Hint
>
> Growth lines work very well for shading animal fur. Just divide the spaces equally in the direction the fur would lay.

Adding Padding to the Petals

1. Couch white carpet and buttonhole twist thread along the edge of the first petal with one strand of silk couching thread or a single strand of white floss. Make the couching stitches very close together, about every $1/16"$ (2mm), to form a firm ridge for the shading stitches to float over. (Fig. 3)

Fig. 2. Foreground petal growth lines.

Fig. 3. Note the couched thread along the petal's edge.

> ### Hint
>
> Make the couching stitches close together to form a stable edge, which will make a crisp line of stitching when the shading stitches are in place. If you are stitching on a very heavy silk ground fabric, there is no need to couch around the edge because the fabric is firm enough to support the crisp edge.

2. The couched thread may or may not conform to the drawn line. If it is off the line, make sure the couched line is outside the drawn line. This is one line that shouldn't show. Extend this couched line halfway up both sides of the petal as shown in the illustration.

3. Couch the padding only on the petal you are going to stitch. Since the couched outline makes the petal a bit bigger, it won't be clear where the edges of subsequent petals start and stop, so outline only the petal you are stitching. When you've finished stitching that petal, add the padding to the next petal.

Selecting Colors

If you have a color photograph or color copy of the design, take it to the store and use it to find matching threads. If you don't have a color copy, use colored pencils to color the design.

DMC floss comes in over 400 colors, so beginners are likely to find colors that match the copy. Intermediate stitchers can use Needlepoint Silk, Splendor, Silk Mori, or Silk Serica - these silks offer a wide selection of colors and are easy to shade. More sophisticated silk shaders might use flat silk.

When I am shading I have one firm rule. I select one or two extra values of a hue and always throw in a white and what I refer to as a "poison"

color. For example, if I am shading with pinks, I add a little lavender.

The colors used in the pink flower are:
• 4 values of Needlepoint Silk pink, from dark to light
   Bright Rose Pink #947
   Carnation Pink #944
   Orchid Lights Range #888
   Orchid Lights Range #887
• Needle Necessities Overdyed Floss, Lavender, Mystique #1481
• Needle Necessities Overdyed Floss, Pink to Orange, Mardi Gras #1547

Hint

I use cut overdyed threads in the areas where one color transitions to the next. I very seldom use the whole thread because the color change is not fast enough for a small petal.

Hint

When choosing values of a hue, it is not necessary to stay in the color family. Adjacent families add variety to the shading and make it more realistic. However, if you are a beginner, I recommend that you select four values of one family.

Color choices are not as critical as changing values. To shade, you must have a mini-

mum of a light, medium, and dark value of each hue. In more sophisticated shading, you can have four or five value changes, and then a value or two of another hue. It is these value changes that lift one petal off the next, making one appear in front of another. In the pink flower, the back petal is dark, with hardly any value changes except at the very center. This accomplishes two things - there is no question where the petal starts and stops and it provides a resting spot for the eye. By that I mean that if the color changes are busy, with no area of almost solid color, the eye won't have anywhere to rest. The eye will flit around without concentrating on the flower and therefore the flower won't appear pleasing to the eye. In all good shading, there must be a resting place - a section, petal, or area with little color change.

Hint

Making color choices is somewhat difficult at first, but becomes more natural with experience. Try making a drawing of the petal/flower and coloring it with colored pencils to use as a guide. When stitching the flower, occasionally examine it at a distance to see the color effect. Often stitchers are too close to the work and don't see the overall effect.

Stitching Random Long and Short

Start with the foreground petal. Each time you stitch a new petal, it should be in front of the unstitched petals. Always start stitching in the center of the petal and work to the right edge, then return to the center and work to the left edge. Don't skip a growth area.

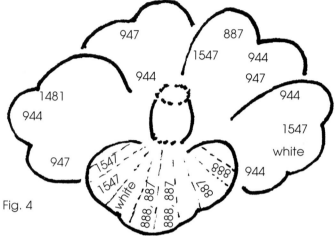

Fig. 4

Row #1

1. You will have already marked growth lines and padded the outer edge of the foreground petal.

2. To shade the foreground petal, start in the center growth area with two strands of Needlepoint Silk #887. Work in one growth area from th edge between two growth lines to the center before starting another. Work the first row along the petal's edge in long (10mm) and short (8mm) stitches. I always take my first stitch in the center of the growth lines and then work to the right side, return to the center, and work to the left. The stitches should not line up but should be randomly long and short. The short stitch should be 2/3 the length of the long stitch. In larger petals you may want to start with three strands, change to two strands, and end with a single strand.

3. The outer edge should form a precise line stitched just over the padding, but the stitches don't have to touch one another. This will also give you a more natural look.

Row #2

1. Still working in the center growth area, make the second row with all long stitches, combining one strand of #887 and #888 in the needle. Be careful not to line up the stitches. The second row stitches should encroach on the first row at the midpoint of the stitches and should extend beyond the long stitches of the first row by at least 3mm or 4mm. Try to make them the same length as the long stitches of the first row. Add one or two stitches of white thread for a highlight.

2. As you near the center, try to hide the needle holes under existing stitches. Try not to pierce the stitches, but slip down between stitches with a slanted needle.

Row #3

1. In the third row, use a thinner thread – one strand of either color. The third row stitches should go down at the midpoint of the second row stitches and extend beyond the second row.

Last Row

1. Stitch the last row of the center growth area with one strand of #888 with one or two stitches of #887 so the color change won't be too abrupt.

2. When you reach the flower center, don't end the stitches in a straight line. Instead, stitch a random line, allowing the ground fabric to peek through. Leave a one-point open space between the center and the petal. This gives a more realistic look to the flower.

3. At the petal edges, you can differentiate the petals with a value change or by leaving exposed ground fabric (a void) the width of the head of a pin. The red flower petals are defined by voids or one-point open spaces. **Note:** *After all the petals were stitched, I couched a metallic to fill the voids between the yellow centers and petals.*

Beyond the First Growth Area

Work between the growth lines from the center to the right side using the same two light values of pink. As you approach the side, use more of

#888 so the side of the petal appears darker than the center. Add an occasional white stitch.

In this example, the growth area to the immediate left of the center is stitched almost entirely with white silk and a splash of #887. The next growth area is stitched with #1547 and touches of white. In the next growth area, I cut overdyed floss #1547 and stitched to the center, again with splashes of white. The last growth area is satin stitched with the very lightest pink cut from the overdyed floss #1547.

After you finish stitching the foreground petal, move to the two petals on either side of the foreground petal. Stitch the last two petals, doing the front one first.

Here's a good example of shading with random long and short. On this flower, you would stitch the small foreground petals first.

Stitch the last petal with a dark value of Needlepoint Silk #947, without changing the value within the petal much. By not changing the color too much, you provide a resting spot for the eye. (When you change color values a lot, there needs to be a place to rest the eye and make the eye comfortable to view the other petals.)

After the flower is stitched, you may feel you need to add a bit of color or white. Stitch a single strand of white silk on top of the pink stitches. Note the white added to the two side petals and the light pink added to the back dark petal. These touches give a realistic effect to the flower.

Hint

Only stitch and think about the color between two growth lines. Stop and check how the colors look. If you want to show something abruptly, such as one petal next to the other, use a high value contrast. If you want to blend more subtly, use very close value changes.

This purple flower was stitched with precise long and short stitches with Needlepoint Silk and overdyed floss.

Purple Flower – Shading with Precise Long and Short Stitches

This technique is not as realistic looking as random long and short, but because of its preciseness it is very appealing to the eye. The petals should be broad like a pansy to take advantage of this method of shading. It does not lend itself to a longer petal flower such as an iris

The photos of the rows of stitches are of a pansy. The pansy would be a very good flower to learn precise long and short stitching because the petals are broader than those in the purple flower. The steps shown in the pansy are the exact steps used to work the purple flower.

Marking Growth Lines on the Petals

1. Start with the petal in the foreground and work backwards until you reach the petal at the back. Refer to page 107 for instructions to mark the growth lines. Use a pencil or chalk pen to draw the same growth lines as in the pink flower.

2. Measure and mark 1cm from the outer edge inward on each growth line. Connect this line to a circle around the front of the petal. In random long and short you stitched from the outer edge to the center of the petal along a growth a line.

Fig. 5

With precise long and short, you stitch completely around the edge of the petal and the longer stitches (10mm) stop at the circle line and alternate with short stitches (7mm). (Fig. 5)

3. Draw two more circular lines about 5mm apart for the subsequent rows.

Selecting Colors

I stitched this purple flower with teaching in mind. The first row is stitched with a dark value of purple to contrast with the ground fabric and to show the long and short stitches. In Row #1, it's critical that the distance between the long stitches at the drawn circle be consistent. The gap should be exactly the distance that will accommodate the stitches in Row #2. By using a dark, high contrast value, you can easily see the distance.

Row #2 is a definite pink so you can see each stitch against the dark purple. The stitches of Row #2 should form a continuous line at the outer edge of the petal. By using a color that contrasts with the purple, you can see every stitch.

Row #3 is stitched in the same color as Row #2.

As you approach the center, the color changes are more subtle. You can see the two adjacent petals have the same coloration but the back petals are just a little more sophisticated. When learning to shade with precise long and short stitches, stitch the second row with a very different color so you can see every stitch. When you are more advanced, use colors closer in value.

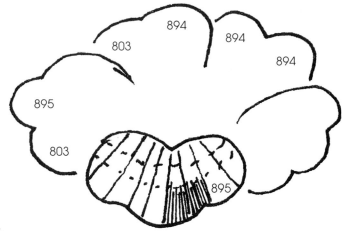

Fig. 6

The colors used in the purple flower are:

- Needlepoint Silk Fuchsia #803
- Purple Needlepoint Silk dark to lightest
  Lilac Range #895
  Lilac Range #894
  Lilac Range #893
  Orchid Lights Range #885
- Needle Necessities
Overdyed Floss
  Harlequin #191, Purple to Pink
  Mystique #1481, Lavenders

Stitching Precise Long and Short

Easy Rules for Precise Long and Short

- Make all stitches parallel to the growth lines.
- Never come up between two stitches. Always pierce the stitch.
- As you approach the center row by row, the thread gets thinner in flat silk. In twisted silks, two rows can be the same thickness but the center row should be thinner than the outer row.
- Row by row, the needle gets smaller.
- The starting and ending stitches are pinhead stitches and should be placed along the outer edge of Row #1.
- Check the thread intervals of each row. Each row must be positioned so the thread of the next row fits between the stitches of the previous row.
- In Rows #1 to #4 always stitch from the center to the right side, then return to the middle and stitch from the center to the left side. This was true in the first petal of the pansy. In the first petal of the purple flower, Rows #1 to #3 were stitched in this manner. The number of rows depends on the size of the petal. In the side petals of the purple flower, the number of rows required to reach the center would be between one and four.

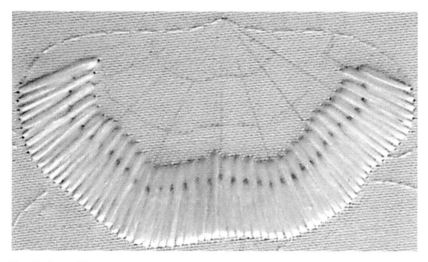
Fig. 7. Row #1.

• The number of strands you use depends on the spacing allowed for the next row. This will vary from student to student and in flower types.

• As you work toward the center, you will have to omit stitches on the ends of the petal. Not all stitches reach the center of the petal. The guidelines direct which stitches reach the middle.

Row #1 (Fig. 7)

1. Start and stop all threads with a pinhead stitch close to the outer edge of the petal. On the foreground petal, stitch two strands of #895. On the pansy shown in the photos, Row #1 is stitched with three strands of white flat silk.

2. Make the first stitch 10mm long in the center of the foreground petal, going over the line. This stitch is clearly illustrated on the first line of the pansy. This stitch was made on the purple flower with three strands of #895 exactly as illustrated on the pansy. This is the only long stitch that goes over the line.

3. To the right of the center stitch, make the second stitch 7mm long. On the pansy, this is done with three strands of flat silk white. On the purple flower it is done with three strands of #895. Note that the stitches along the edges of the flower do not necessarily touch each other. This gives a more realistic look. On the purple flower, the whole first row on the foreground petal is dark purple.

4. From this point forward, alternate a long 10mm stitch and a short 7mm stitch, working to the right edge of the flower. All the long stitches should end on the circular line and should be an equal distance apart. The short stitches should form a line all the way around the flower. The openings between the long stitches should be the exact size to accommodate a smaller thread in the second row of stitches. Start with three strands of stranded silk on the outer row and decrease the number of strands as the rows approach the center of the flower. If you use three strands

of Needlepoint Silk or flat silk in Row #1, you might make Row #2 with two strands of Needlepoint Silk or $2\frac{1}{2}$ strands of flat silk, depending on the size of the petal and the opening between the long stitches. Therefore, when starting to make the first few stitches, make sure the smaller number of strands used in Row #2 will fit into the openings created by the long stitches in Row #1.

Hint

When I am stitching Row #1, I periodically lay the thread I am going to use for Row #2 between two long stitches to see if the opening will accommodate the thread thickness.

Hint

I cannot emphasize this enough. *The long stitches should be an equal distance apart.* Row #2 stitches must fit into the openings left by the long stitches, so use great care to make the openings an equal distance apart to insure that all Row #2 stitches fit precisely between the long stitches of Row #1 and all the stitches follow the growth lines.

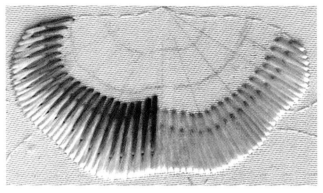

Fig. 8. Row #2.

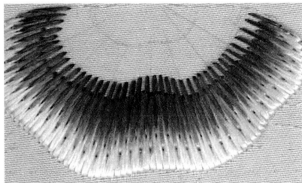

Fig. 9. Row #3.

5. Return to the center and stitch to the left edge. It is very important that when each growth line is met, the stitch, long or short, runs parallel to the growth line. To accomplish this, adjust the width of the stitches along the outer edge, thus leaving space between the stitches. The stitches on the outer edge of the petal should just touch each other or be very close without crowding. This gives a more realistic effect.

6. Before going on to Row #2, review Row #1. The length of the long and short stitches should be consistent and all the long stitches should end on the circular line. The openings created between the long stitches should be equal. When the stitches come to a growth line, they should be parallel with the growth line. There will probably be spaces between stitches on the outer edge of the petal.

Row #2 (Fig. 8)

1. Start Row #2 stitches at the midpoint of the short stitches in Row #1, splitting the threads of the first row stitches. Make the center stitch 8mm long.

Row #2 in the pansy is $2^{1}/_{2}$ strands of purple flat silk. On the purple flower, Row #2 is two strands of overdyed floss #1481. I always recommend that in the first petal the first and second rows be of a great value contrast or a change of color so you can see both rows clearly.

2. All other stitches in Row #2 are 7mm long. Stitch to the middle area between the two circular lines. Always stitch Row #2 from the center to the right side of the petal, then return to the center and stitch the left side of the petal.

3. It is important to end the stitches to form a circular line. Make the stitches an equal distance apart at this circular line and parallel to the growth lines. This is done to assure that Row #3 stitches will fit between the openings created by the stitches in Row #2. Row #3 stitches will be thinner than those in Row #2, so make sure the openings remain consistent. Note how the outer edge of this row forms a circular line.

4. Review Row #2. The stitches

should all be the same length – 7mm (except the center 8mm stitch). There should be an equal opening between each stitch on the circular line and the stitches should be parallel to the growth lines and form a circle on the outer edge.

Row #3 (Fig. 9)

1. Start Row #3 at the midpoint of the long stitches from Row #1. Stitch it with two strands of darker purple flat silk. On the purple flower Row #3 is stitched with one strand of overdyed floss #191 to show primarily the pink shades.

Hint

In the first three rows of the purple flower, I used distinct color changes so the rows would be very visible. For your first petal in this technique it is helpful to use three hues or three values of one color far enough apart to allow you to see the separate rows of stitching. As you gain proficiency at shading, you can use colors closer together in value.

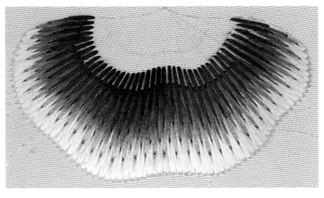

Fig. 10. Row #4.

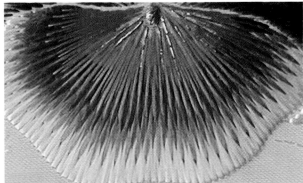

Fig. 11. Row #5.

2. Repeat the same stitching process as for Row #2, starting in the middle of the petal, but make the stitches from the midpoint of the Row #1 long stitches to reach the circular line drawn on the fabric.

3. Make all stitches the same length (7mm to 8mm). They should extend beyond the Row #2 stitches in the middle of the flower. Make sure they are parallel to the growth lines. Remember that the spaces between stitches must accommodate a thinner thread in Row #4.

4. When you reach the outer edge of the petal, some of the stitches in Row #3 may end on the edge of the petal and won't reach the center of the flower. The photo shows the ending of these stitches. Not all stitches reach the center of the flower.

Row #4 (Fig. 10)

1. Row #4 on the pansy is stitched with one strand of a darker value of purple flat silk. Row #4 on the purple flower is stitched with one strand of Needlepoint Silk #895.

Hint

It is important to understand that when you are shading with Needlepoint Silk and overdyed floss, you cannot achieve the thinness of thread that flat silk affords. With other threads, the center rows of stitches are thinner than the outer rows but they do not allow the flexibility that flat silk does. Flat silk also gives the highest light play so a flower stitched in all white gives the illusion of shading, which is just the refraction of the light.

2. Make the stitches 7mm to 8mm in length, from the midpoint of Row #2 to extend 2mm to 3mm beyond the Row #3 stitches. Not all stitches will go to the center of the flower, some will end on the side of the petal. Make the stitches run parallel to the growth lines.

3. On the purple flower, Row #4 completes the petal and is stitched in a random style to leave a jagged edge and a small part of the ground fabric showing at the center.

Row #5 (Fig. 11)

1. Stitch Row #5 on the pansy randomly, with some stitches using a half strand of yellow flat silk and some stitches using a fourth strand of flat silk. It is most important on this row that the stitches not end precisely at the center of the flower. They should be very open, in varying stitch lengths. Work the stitches out of order, filling the area but letting a little of the ground fabric show through. This gives the illusion that it is a delicate center. This is a very good place to use a change of color such as the yellow on the purple in the pansy. You could also add a little fine metallic gold.

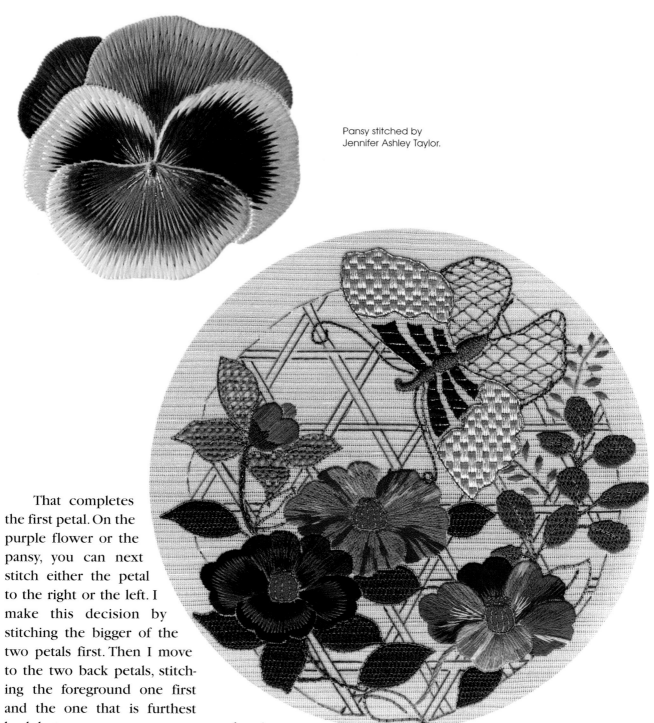

Pansy stitched by
Jennifer Ashley Taylor.

That completes the first petal. On the purple flower or the pansy, you can next stitch either the petal to the right or the left. I make this decision by stitching the bigger of the two petals first. Then I move to the two back petals, stitching the foreground one first and the one that is furthest back last.

On the other four petals of the purple flower, I used more than one color for Row #1. This requires a needle threaded for each color. Stitch in precise steps – don't stitch a pocket of color and then fill each side of the color. When you change colors, thread that color in a needle, park the first color out of the way, stitch the new color, then park that color and resume stitching with the first color.

The center of the purple flower was stitched in the same way as the center of the pink flower (see page 105).

"Harmony" shows three kinds of shading – random long and short, precise long and short, and split stitch. I used gold work cloud filling to decorate the back wings of the butterfly. I stitched the front wings in raised couching, but with needlepoint threads instead of metallic. I did the leaves in a variety of needlepoint stitches.

"Climbing Elegance" Bell Pull – Shading on Canvas

Stitched shading doesn't have to be done on fabric. This bell pull design is on needlepoint canvas that is shaded with the same techniques used on fabric. When stitching on canvas, use a sharp chenille needle and pierce the canvas threads when necessary.

The large pink flowers were shaded in random long and short stitches, using the same methods as the pink flower on page 107.

This piece illustrates the exquisite shading that's possible on needlepoint canvas.

The lovely bell pull shows the combination of shading techniques and needlepoint stitches on needlepoint canvas instead of fabric.

Design by Bettie Ray Designs.
Stitched by Dorothy Goldstick.

The padded satin stitch edges give the appearance of flipped over petals.

The edges of the flower that appear to turn over were stitched first in a padding stitch with four or five strands of the lightest pink values of Needlepoint Silk. Start with a waste knot and a pinhead stitch in the area to be stitched. Lay four or five stitches in the center of the area *in the opposite direction* of the satin stitches that will form this area. These are called "self-padding" stitches because the area is padded with the same thread as will be stitched on top.

Always make padding stitches 1mm inside the outline of the design, perpendicular to the top satin stitches. Padding stitches are laid stitches, meaning you don't put any threads on the back of the work. When you bring up the needle on the left side of the motif and go down on the right side, you make the return stitch by coming up on the same right side and going down on the left. A satin stitch brings all the stitches up on one side and takes all the stitches down on the other side of the motif. This puts an equal amount of thread on the front and back of the work. A laid stitch puts all the thread on the front. This is important in padding because you only want to pad the front of the work, not the back.

Make all the padding stitches inside the black edges that define the motif. Don't extend them out to the ends of the motif. After the padding is in place, satin stitch the portion of the petal that appears to be turned over.

The edges could also have been lifted by couching buttonhole twist around them before padding and stitching the satin stitches. The satin stitches would then have extended out to cover the couched outline.

Next mark the growth lines in each petal. In this example, the growth lines were stitched with a running stitch of one strand of the lightest pink silk and were never removed. In the dark areas, the silk thread was covered up and in the lighter areas, the silk peeks through. The petals are stitched with random long and short. On some petals, a running stitch of dark red metallic braid adds definition and separates the petals.

The center of this flower is stitched in a tent stitch with dark pink silk (combining needlepoint and embroidery stitches in one motif).

Note how the background stitch flows into basketweave stitches near the flower petals.

Embroidery techniques were blended with a variety of needlepoint stitches on this piece. The purple flowers feature bullion stitches, the yellow flowers show needle lace and satin edges.

The background stitch choice in this piece is interesting. Since bell pulls can be very long (this one is 40"), the background stitch shouldn't be a tiny repeat pattern that would take a lifetime to stitch. However, there are many small areas around the flowers that won't accommodate a large stitch. In this case, the stitcher switched to a basketweave stitch when she neared the dense flowers and randomly combined the two stitches on the edges. If you try this method, don't make a precise line from one stitch to the other – let the two stitches meld together in a planned random look.

Another example of random long and short stitches on canvas.
"Lazy Cat" from Tapestry Tent Designs.
Stitched by Eleanor Gibson.

On a large piece like this I advise that you work on the background as you go. Don't leave all the background stitching until the end or you may abandon the project before you finish. In any project, it's not the finishing that counts, it's the enjoyment you get from stitching. I have enjoyed some pieces so much I hated to have them end!

The face was done with a tent stitch. The whiskers were made by covering a fine wire with buttonhole stitches and the end of the wire imbedded in the canvas. The cat's body was done in random long and short. The rocks were done in the same stitch but in color values more defined.

GALLERY OF DESIGNS

The "Moon Princess" was stitched on uneven Ro fabric with a variety of Japanese embroidery, needlepoint, and embroidery stitches.

Note the sweep of the hair. I couched it down after I completed all the stitching, so it rests on top of the completed work.

There is a wonderful Japanese fairy tale about an old bamboo cutter and his wife. He cut down a bamboo glowing with light and inside he found a beautiful baby girl. Each day he found a glowing bamboo and cut it down and each was filled with gold to buy his daughter lovely silks. People came from far and wide to see her dazzling beauty. Even though royal princes came to woo her, she never wed and spent a happy time with the old couple. One night as she was gazing at the moon she started to weep and the old couple asked her why. "I am from the moon and must return." At midnight on the 15th of August a cloud of light appeared from a full moon and with a tearful goodbye, she stepped onto the cloud of

I couched on curls as the final finishing touch.

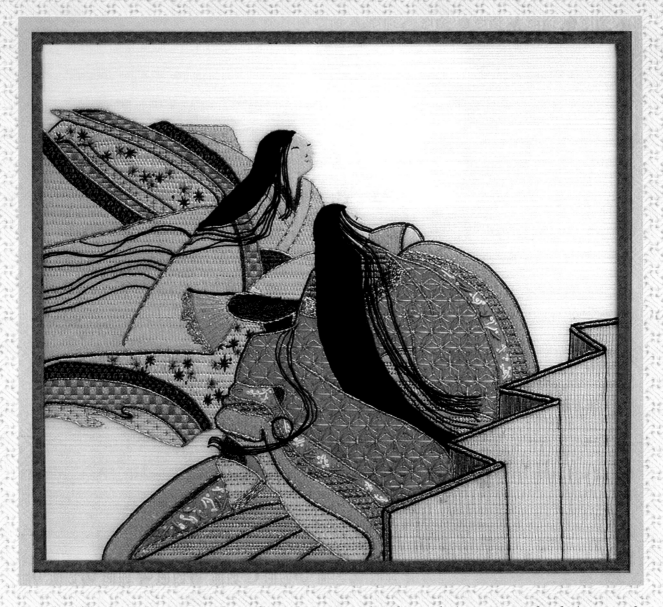

I stitched "The Sisters" on uneven Ro, utilizing Japanese embroidery techniques, counted techniques, and appliquéd netting to form the screen.

light and rose up to the heavens to return to the moon. Whenever you see the Moon Princess pictured in Japan, you see her from the back as she returns to the moon. This fascinating story inspired my "Moon Princess" adaptation.

I stitched "Moon Princess" on uneven Ro fabric so I could combine counted stitches, embroidery stitches, and couching.

I stitched the hair in a Japanese embroidery technique. I laid a horizontal foundation of satin stitches across the area of the hair. This foundation ran perpendicular to the way hair would naturally fall. The foundation stitches are dense enough so that when I placed stitches on top of the flat silk, the foundation didn't part. I stitched the hair completely with flat silk and then

couched perle cotton #12 and #8 from the top of the head to the bottom of the hair. I left a small opening between the rows of couching to make it look like strands of hair.

I couched black perle cotton with one strand of black six-stranded cotton. I couched the two outer edges first, then couched down the middle. From this point on, I just kept dividing the open spaces in half.

"The Chinese Lady" was inspired by a doubled-sided screen in my house. I stitched it on uneven Ro and embellished it with a variety of threads and techniques.

The foundation barely peeked through between the rows of couching to look like hair. I couched the curls on after I completed the rest of the stitching on "Moon Princess."

In traditional needlepoint, the flowers adorning the kimono would be stitched first and the background stitched behind them. However, there is another way to stitch this area. I laid a vertical foundation the length of the kimono and tied it down with a lattice of thin metallic thread, then stitched the flowers on top, placing them where they balanced the best.

I had such fun stitching the "Moon Princess" I wanted to try another lady with many kimonos. As I was looking for inspiration I thought it would be even more fun to have two ladies. "The Sisters," with their long flowing hair and layered kimonos, appeared to be perfect for translation into stitches. I stitched this adaptation on uneven Ro with a combination of needlepoint stitches and techniques from Japanese embroidery. Decorating the kimonos with different stitches and balancing the colors were part of the challenge of the design.

*Notice the delicate outline
between the fingers.*

I stitched the screen in the front by first appliqueing a netting to the Ro and then laying #1 gold in straight lines on every
other row of holes in the Ro. Then I couched the netting and #1
gold with silk couching thread in a linear pattern. I couched the
folds in a much heavier braid to make them more prominent and
appear as folds.

This elegant Chinese courtesan, with her delicate face and
hands, was a challenge to stitch. After experimenting on the
hands, I chose to outline the hands and each finger with a very
thin 100-weight silk. I very carefully couched along the edges of
the hand and each finger. The color of the silk was critical – it
needed to be just a value darker than the flesh but dark enough
to define the fingers. Once I completed the outlining I stitched
each finger and palm in a satin stitch with a half strand of flat silk.
I needed a slight value change for a more realistic look. When I
completed stitching the hand, I stitched red flat silk over the flesh
color to look like nail polish.

The inspiration for "The Dresses" was an old English pattern book. I stitched it on Sha fabric in a variety of needlepoint stitches and threads and added appliqués.

Wearing beautiful clothes has long been a standing tradition, so embellishing clothes with stitches seemed a very natural thing to do. I stitched "The Dresses" on Sha fabric, which gave me the opportunity to use diagonal as well as vertical stitches. However, Sha does not lend itself to the tent stitch. It is not a true even fabric in most cases. It is 100% silk, so silk threads glide over the ground fabric with ease.

It is always fun to add bits of beads, lace, or any found object to embellish a piece (note the lace on the sleeves). Use your imagination and stitch a motif for the fun of it, adding your own personal touches.

This dress illustrates needlepoint stitches combined with Japanese cord embellished with lace.

Here you see precise needlepoint stitches combined with appliquéd lace.

I stitched this white flower with flat silk in random long and short, then overstitched with one strand of Japanese gold thread and a half strand of pink flat silk. The shine of the flat silk helps define the petals.

I stitched this white flower on uneven Ro ground fabric. Since this is a rather soft ground fabric, it will not hold an edge well, so it is best to reinforce the petal edge by couching white carpet and buttonhole twist around the front edge and halfway up each side edge. I divided the flower petals into growth areas exactly like the pink flower on page 109. I did the first stitches in the growth line at the outer edge with two strands of flat silk and as I approached the center, I used one strand, then a half strand.

I stitched the flower in white flat silk thread. Then I overstitched one strand of #1 Japanese gold on the white and added pink flat silk as an accent in the center of the flower.

If you would like to stitch with fewer strands, repeat the process with a half strand of flat silk. Suga can actually be counted, so the center of a shaded flower could be stitched with as few as two or three suga. This is a very fine thread that works wonderfully to overstitch at the center of a flower. As the stitches reach the center, they should be smaller in diameter and using flat silk allows for very fine and delicate stitches.

The more you work with flat silk, the easier it gets. It takes some practice, but the results are worth the added work.

I stitched this striking red flower with precise long and short petals with counted techniques and gold work on patterned Sha fabric.

This red flower illustrates how difficult it is to distinguish one row from another when the rows are stitched in one color with close value changes. The petals are large and require four or five strands for the first row and an extended stitch length. Adjust the thickness and length of the stitches to the flower size and add the white accent after the flower is completed.

"Morning Glories" makes a wonderful palette for shading. This piece includes some random long and short, some precise long and short, outline stitching, and the split stitch.

I have always been fascinated by the coloring in flowers and spend a lot of time perusing seed catalogs to study the coloration in different blossoms. When I decided to tackle a morning glory piece, I studied the magazines and photos on seed packets, which led me to experiment with different types of shading. I stitched the flower in the lower right corner with precise long and short and the remaining flowers with random long and short, split stitch, and a combination of random long and short and stem stitch. Where the thin dark blue lines are very prominent, stem stitch seems to emphasize the lines and makes an impact on the flower.

Approach each flower with a critical eye. See how they grow, what color or value of that color will produce the most effect. Examine where the flower joins the stem. The green stem should come forward of the juncture because the flower grows out of the stem. You can bring the stem forward by use of color or by the texture of the stitch. Morning glories have a very delicate growth out of the stem, so a simple flat stitch was needed. Stems must appear strong enough to support the flower, yet delicate enough to remain true to the nature of the flower.

A close-up of the shading stitches made with Needlepoint Silk.

The very stylized leaves in "Morning Glories" were stitched with various counted or needlepoint stitches. Because the piece was stitched on uneven Ro fabric, all the counted stitches had to be linear. It is extremely difficult to stitch a diagonal stitch on uneven Ro because it is not a true even weave fabric. It is also a challenge because the holes are not a uniform distance apart. This adds a great deal of interest to the piece.

Because counted stitches are relatively open and tend to float off the design, I weight them by couching gold around their edges. This forms an edge on the leaves and adds richness to the embroidery. Leaves with denser stitches have well defined edges and may not need to have the edges couched. The value of the green color makes an impact on the edge of a leaf. Light-value edges need to be defined, where dark-edged leaves have a high contrast with the light ground fabric and appear well defined.

I shaded the butterfly wings with French knots tightly stitched together. I couched the antennae with crinkle. The small butterfly features one stitched wing and one wing outlined with running backstitches.

Designed by Jennifer Ashley Taylor.

Shading with French knots is a great technique that works beautifully with fluffy yarn to make charming teddy bears, cuddly cats, and bunnies.

This butterfly was used on my PBS television program, so the color values of the twisted flat silk threads are exaggerated to show the change in value and to illustrate how to move from one hue or value to the next by mixing the new color with the old color. This adds dimension to the shading. The three values of flat silk exaggerate the change in value so the shading becomes very definite. If you were doing this butterfly, you might like a more subtle change in value.

On the orange petals of this flower, I used chain stitches for shading.

There are many ways to shade. You can use rows of chain stitching as in the simple flower shown above. Stitch a row of chain stitches around one petal, then change colors or values as the subsequent rows approach the center of the petal.

The blue petals on either side of the flower are stitched in random long and short, illustrating that combining techniques in the same flower can be successful.

The completed flower shows the orange petals shaded with chain stitches and the blue petals shaded with random long and short.

I stitched "Temari Balls" on uneven Ro with a variety of threads and techniques.

On one of my trips to Japan, I began to collect temari balls – decorative balls mothers make to give to their daughters for the New Year. Traditionally they were made with old bits of threads, some pulled from raveled cloth. Today the balls are made with lots of brightly colored threads and they are sold all over Japan as souvenirs. They are usually decorated in geometric patterns. I added the butterflies and cord to tie the design together.

The stitches are a combination of counted needlepoint, bargello, embroidery techniques, and couching.

"Jeweled Flowers." I stitched this design on patterned Sha fabric with gold work and Japanese embroidery techniques.

In Japanese design, it is common to see circles with inner motifs. "Jeweled Flowers" grew from this circle concept but I made it more interesting by not having all the circles show completely. The flowers in jewel tones were stitched in padded satin stitches. The unique gold background behind the flowers was stitched in gold work back and forth techniques. The crescent shapes were done by overstitching the pattern woven into the Sha fabric. The gold reaches the edges of the circle, but there is always one point of open space at the circle edge, then the gold also fades into the flowers.

ABOUT THE AUTHOR

Photo courtesy of Detroit Public Television.

Shay Pendray has studied Japanese embroidery for over 18 years and has had the privilege of studying with four sensei (teachers). Her fascination with the methods and results led her to become the driving force in bringing Japanese embroidery to the United States.

Shay is certified in canvas work by the Embroiderers' Guild of America and is a teacher, lecturer, designer, and host of the popular long-running PBS television series *The Embroidery Studio*. She currently produces and hosts the highly-rated new PBS series *Needle Arts Studio 2*. She has taught over 150 seminars on embroidery and business, has authored four books and is the owner of Needle Arts, Inc., a retail store that specializes in needlework products.

Visit her Web site at www.shaypendray.com. You can e-mail her at shaypendray@worldnet.att.net.

INDEX

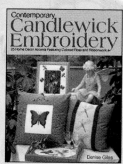

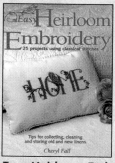

Needlework Art
you can create

Crewel Embroidery
by Sue Hawkins
Recreate the shapes and textures of crewel embroidery through instruction, templates, and a stitch library with projects including pin cushions, purses, and more.

Hardcover • 8-1/4 x 11 • 128 pages
90 2-color illus. • 80 color photos, 25 4-color
Item# 41121 • $27.95

Beth Russell's Traditional Needlepoint
by Beth Russell
This book of traditional stitching designs is filled with easy-to-learn instructions, full-color charts and photos, and is ideal for stitchers of all skill levels.

Softcover • 8-1/2 x 11-1/4 • 128 pages
68 color photos, 42 pages color charts
Item# 41103 • $19.95

The Complete Needlepoint Guide
400+ Needlepoint Stitches
by Susan Sturgeon-Roberts
Hundreds of finely-detailed stitch diagrams and more than 300 photos make this book the definitive reference for the novice or expert needle artist, from cross stitch to fine embroidery. Veteran needle artist Susan Sturgeon-Roberts offers a complete introduction to the art of needleworking, discussing the finer points of canvases, yarns, and the various materials available for creating beautiful examples of homespun art.

Softcover • 8-1/4 x 10-7/8 • 192 pages
400+ b&w photos, 550 illustrations • 48 color photos
Item# CNG • $24.95

Gifts to Cross Stitch
by B.J. McDonald
Easily create more than 50 gifts for anniversaries, new babies, weddings, graduations, and more relying on gorgeous photographs, easy-to-follow instructions, and detailed charts. Confidently follow designs compiled from the most talented cross stitch designers, including those from such well-known manufacturers as DMC, Coats & Clark, Charles Craft, and more.

Softcover • 8-1/4 x 10-7/8 • 144 pages
75 cross stitch charts • 100 color photos & illus.
Item# XSTCH • $24.99

Native American Cross Stitch
by Julie Hasler
Unique designs inspired by the art and culture of Native Americans. Projects include dream catchers and a Navajo rug.

Softcover • 8-1/4 x 11 • 128 pages
8 pages of stitch motifs • 35 color photos, 25 color charts
Item# 41054 • $19.99

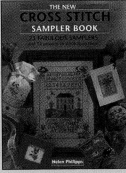

The New Cross Stitch Sampler Book
by Helen Philipps
72 projects; gift tags and mini pictures.

Softcover • 8-3/4 x 11-1/2 • 128 pages
30 color photos, 30 color charts
Item# 41395 • $17.99

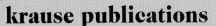